BEST OF

Barcelona

Damien Simonis

Best of Barcelona
2nd edition – February 2005
First published – May 2002

Published by Lonely Planet Publications Pty Ltd
ABN 36 005 607 983

Australia	Head Office, Locked Bag 1, Footscray, Vic 3011
	☎ 03 8379 8000 fax 03 8379 8111
	✉ talk2us@lonelyplanet.com.au
USA	150 Linden St, Oakland, CA 94607
	☎ 510 893 8555 toll free 800 275 8555
	fax 510 893 8572
	✉ info@lonelyplanet.com
UK	72–82 Rosebery Avenue, London EC1R 4RW
	☎ 020 7841 9000 fax 020 7841 9001
	✉ go@lonelyplanet.co.uk

This title was commissioned in Lonely Planet's London office and produced by: **Commissioning Editor** Heather Dickson **Coordinating Editor** Sarah Bailey **Coordinating Cartographers** Corey Hutchison, Jenny Jones **Layout Designer** Laura Jane **Managing Editor** Bruce Evans **Managing Cartographer** Mark Griffiths **Cover Designers** Pepi Bluck, Wendy Wright **Project Manager** Rachel Imeson **Mapping Development** Paul Piaia **Thanks to** Stefanie Di Trocchio, Fiona Christie, Imogen Franks, Melanie Dankel, Judith Bamber

© Lonely Planet Publications Pty Ltd 2005.

Photographs by Lonely Planet Images and Neil Setchfield except for the following: p5, p8, p9, p11, p13, p19, p20, p21, p23, p32, p34, p36, p37, p43, p44, p51, p53, p55, p56, p61, p62, p68, p69, p90, p95, p96, p103, p106, p107, p110, p111 Martin Hughes/Lonely Planet Images, p22 Damien Simonis/Lonely Planet Images, p25 Geoff Stringer/Lonely Planet Images, p49 Martin Moos/Lonely Planet Images, p50 Guy Moberly/Lonely Planet Images, p73 Oliver Strewe/ Lonely Planet Images, p105 Pascale Beroujon/Lonely Planet Images, p109 Christopher Groenhout/Lonely Planet Images. **Cover photograph** La Sagrada Familia, designed by Antoni Gaudi, Oliver Strewe/Lonely Planet Images. All images are copyright of the photographers unless otherwise indicated. Many of the images in this guide are available for licensing from Lonely Planet Images:
✉ www.lonelyplanetimages.com

ISBN 1 74059 475 4

Printed by Markono Print Media Pte Ltd, Singapore

Acknowledgements Barcelona Metro Map © 2004 TMB

HOW TO USE THIS BOOK

Colour-Coding & Maps

Each chapter has a colour code along the banner at the top of the page which is also used for text and symbols on maps (eg all venues reviewed in the Highlights chapter are orange on the maps). The fold-out maps inside the front and back covers are numbered from 1 to 8. All sights and venues in the text have map references; eg, (6, B2) means Map 6, grid reference B2. See p128 for map symbols.

Prices

Multiple prices listed with reviews (eg €10/5) usually indicate adult/concession admission to a venue. Concession prices can include senior, student, child or coupon discounts. Meal cost and room rate categories are listed at the start of the Eating and Sleeping chapters, respectively.

Text Symbols

☎	telephone
✉	address
🖳	email/website address
€	admission
☽	opening hours
Ⓜ	metro
Ⓡ	FGC
🚌	bus
Ⓟ	parking available
♿	wheelchair access
✗	on site/nearby eatery
♣	child-friendly venue
Ⓥ	good vegetarian selection

Contents

INTRODUCING BARCELONA	5
NEIGHBOURHOODS	6
ITINERARIES	7
HIGHLIGHTS	8
La Sagrada Família	8
Museu Picasso	10
Museu Nacional d'Art de Catalunya	11
Església de Santa Maria del Mar	12
Museu d'Història de la Ciutat	13
L'Aquàrium	14
Catedral	15
La Pedrera	16
Casa Batlló	17
Fundació Joan Miró	18
La Rambla	19
Parc Güell	20
Museu del Futbol Club Barcelona	21
Museu Marítim	22
Museu-Monestir de Pedralbes	23
Palau de la Música Catalana	24
Parc de la Ciutadella	25
Palau Güell	26

SIGHTS & ACTIVITIES	27
Museums & Galleries	27
Churches & Cathedrals	31
Plaças, Parks & Public Spaces	33
Public Art	36
Notable Buildings & Monuments	38
Quirky Barcelona	41
Barcelona for Children	42

OUT & ABOUT	45
Walking Tours	45
Day Trips	49
Organised Tours	51

SHOPPING	52
Fashion, Clothes & Shoes	53
Design, Homeware & Gifts	56
Food & Drink	57
Books & Music	59

Antiques & Crafts	60
Department Stores & Malls	61
Jewellery, Perfume & Accessories	62
Markets	63
For Children	64
Specialist Stores	64

EATING	66
La Rambla	68
Barri Gòtic	69
El Raval & Poble Sec	73
La Ribera	75
L'Eixample	78
Gràcia	80
La Barceloneta	81

ENTERTAINMENT	83
Bars & Pubs	84
Dance Clubs	87
Cinemas	88
Rock, Jazz & Blues	90
Flamenco	91
Classical Music, Opera, Dance & Theatre	92
Gay & Lesbian Barcelona	91
Sport	94

SLEEPING	96
Deluxe	97
Top End	98
Mid-Range	100
Budget	102

ABOUT BARCELONA	103
History	103
Environment	106
Government & Politics	106
Economy	107
Society & Culture	108
Arts	108

DIRECTORY	111
INDEX	123
MAP LEGEND	128

From the Publisher

AUTHOR

Damien Simonis

Damien first made the acquaintance of Barcelona in 1990, but would not renew it until eight years later, when on assignment for Lonely Planet. What a place! The medieval lanes of the Barri Gòtic, the chic boulevards of the central Eixample (the Quadrat d'Or or Golden Square), the endless restaurants, bars and terraces, the seaside location and the bicultural ambience – it all struck a deep chord. Within no time he had a room in a top-floor Gran Via apartment and in the following years Barcelona gradually became a second home.

There are many people in Barcelona who, whether they know it or not, have helped out in bigger and smaller ways. They include Edith López García, María Barbosa Pérez (and Enric), Silvia Folch, Susan Kempster, Michael van Laake and Rocio Vázquez, Susana Pellicer (and the Ceba gang), Ottobrina Voccoli, Teresa Moreno Quintana, Nicole Neuefeind, Armin Teichmann, José María Toro and Eduard Antonijuan (the world's friendliest bankers!), Stephan Rundel, Simona Volonterio, Oscar Elias, Steven Muller and Veronika Brinkmann, Núria Vilches, Xavi Orfells, Geoff Leaver-Heaton (and Lola and little Natalia), John Rochlin, Peter Sotirakis, and Damien Harris.

The 1st edition of this book was written by Martin Hughes.

PHOTOGRAPHER

Neil Setchfield

Neil Setchfield spends four months a year travelling the world, and his pictures have appeared in over 120 magazines and newspapers worldwide. Barcelona – which Neil has visited over 20 times in the last five years – is one of his favourite cities. So much so that his five-year plan is to relocate there (or nearby) permanently. While shooting for Lonely Planet, Neil sampled tripe from Mercat de la Boqueria, set fire to absinthe in El Raval's Bar Marsella, and sat alone in Camp Nou stadium dreaming of Spurs winning the Champions League! Neil currently lives in London.

SEND US YOUR FEEDBACK

We love to hear from travellers – your comments keep us on our toes and help make our books better. Our well-travelled team reads every word on what you loved or loathed about this book. Although we cannot reply individually to postal submissions, we always guarantee that your feedback goes straight to the appropriate authors, in time for the next edition – and the most useful submissions are rewarded with a free book. To send us your updates – and find out about Lonely Planet events, newsletters and travel news – visit our award-winning website: 🖳 **www.lonelyplanet.com/feedback.**

Note: We may edit, reproduce and incorporate your comments in Lonely Planet products such as guidebooks, websites and digital products, so let us know if you don't want your comments reproduced or your name acknowledged. For a copy of our privacy policy visit 🖳 www.lonelyplanet.com/privacy.

Introducing Barcelona

'Barcelona is the best city in Europe.' The remark came not from the city's mayor, but from an Italian TV news director in that other Mediterranean beauty queen, Venice. Praise indeed! The Mediterranean metropolis is a rare blend. A hard-working populace makes Spain's second city an economic powerhouse. It is also a hedonist's paradise. Fiercely proud of its Catalan identity, it promotes itself as a sparkling international centre. With immigration rapidly on the rise, it is on the way to becoming one of Spain's focal points of multi-cultural experimentation.

From Gothic to Gaudí, the architecture will make you swoon. Urban projects reflect the city's openness to cutting-edge creators like Frank Gehry and Jean Nouvel. World-class museums with collections ranging from Picasso to the latest in contemporary art nourish the soul. But what makes Barcelona glitter with a touch of wickedness is its buzzing, dynamic present. Central Barcelona offers an extraordinary concentration of restaurants, bars and clubs – and provides the perfect hangover cure with beaches and marinas. Visited by a variegated urban fauna taking in everyone from rock-and-roll Rollerbladers to domino-playing pensioners, the waterfront could be LA on the Med. Leading names in fashion and food lend it a tingling Now! feeling.

It's a mind-blowing cocktail, made with equal measures of culture, style and passion, and with a dash of petty street crime to give it some zest. It is unimaginable until you arrive, unbelievable while you are here and unforgettable after you've left – if you leave.

Mushrooming chimneypots on the roof of Gaudí's La Pedrera (p16)

Neighbourhoods

Barcelona is compact, occupying a plain between an amphitheatre of hills and the Mediterranean on Spain's northeast coast. **Tibidabo** is the highest peak of the inland range. This guide concentrates on an inverted T, with the horizontal line running along the coast from the Olympic hill of **Montjuïc** in the southwest to **Port Olímpic** and beyond in the northeast. **La Rambla** (p19) runs perpendicular to the coastline. On either side of this boulevard stretch the **Ciutat Vella** (Old Town), divided into **El Raval** to the southwest, the **Barri Gòtic** (Gothic Quarter) to the northeast and **La Ribera** beyond.

Off the Beaten Track

Sick of lining up to view Barcelona's monuments? Want to get a look at lesser-known sides of the city? Locals with a penchant for walks, running in the woods and mountain biking head for the **Parc de Collserola** (p33), a vast green lung spread out over the hills that form the city's inland backdrop. Otherwise, take a stroll among the cacti of the **Jardins de Mossèn Costa i Llobera** (p33), one of many gardens scattered across Montjuïc, or the nearby **Jardí Botànic** (p33).

The medieval streets of the Barri Gòtic are lined with historic buildings and wonderful places to eat and drink. Across the noisy Via Laietana, La Ribera is home to fascinating relics and the **Museu Picasso** (p10). Between the museum and the expansive **Parc de la Ciutadella** (p25) is the too-cool-for-school district of **El Born**, which is a magnet for style and a hub of exuberant nightlife. El Raval, long the toughest and poorest part of central Barcelona, remains dodgy in parts but is regenerating, with major art centres like the **Museu d'Art Contemporani de Barcelona** (Macba; p28) and a blossoming of bars. Beyond, the hill of Montjuïc is dotted with gardens, museums like the **Fundació Joan Miró** (p18) and Olympic installations.

Fun, games and model planes at Fòrum 2004 (p37)

The seaside starts with the rejuvenated **Port Vell** (Old Port) and moves northeast to the working-class district of **La Barceloneta**, known for its seafood eateries. Beyond lie the Port Olímpic marina, a string of beaches and the waterfront development known alternatively as **Diagonal Mar** and **El Fòrum**.

La Rambla leads inland to **Plaça de Catalunya**, which marks the boundary between Barcelona's old and new quarters. Passeig de Gràcia continues the line and is the main artery of **l'Eixample** (the Extension), which is home to most of Barcelona's Modernista architecture and connects with the district of **Gràcia**, a separate town until the late 19th century.

Itineraries

Between museums that boggle with their brilliance and buildings that confound with their creativity, Barcelona has enough sights to keep you exploring for months. Most are easy to reach on foot or by metro.

Articket (€15), available at tourist offices, gives admission to six major sights, including the Museu Nacional d'Art de Catalunya (MNAC), the Fundació Joan Miró and La Pedrera.

Day One

Ramble along **La Rambla** (p19) and wander through the medieval marvel of the Barri Gòtic to the **Museu Picasso** (p10) in La Ribera, before retiring to lunch around Passeig del Born. Catch the metro to **La Sagrada Família** (p8) and then, after a sunset stroll along the beaches, steer into La Barceloneta for some succulent seafood.

Lowlights

Even in Barcelona some things are less than perfect, such as:

- The stench of human urine and doggie doings in parts of the old town
- Noisy hotel rooms in the heart of town
- Pickpockets and bag-snatchers
- The thundering, traffic-choked Via Laietana

Day Two

Start with the Modernista masterpieces of Passeig de Gràcia, taking in Gaudí's **La Pedrera** (p16) and **Casa Batlló** (p17). Browse the nearby boutiques and have lunch at the **Cerveseria Catalana** (p78). Head for Montjuïc for an afternoon of art at the **MNAC** (p11) and **Fundació Joan Miró** (p18), followed by dinner and drinks in El Raval.

Day Three

Give the Barri Gòtic closer inspection, taking in the **Catedral** (p15) and the **Museu d'Història de la Ciutat** (p13). For a change of pace, giddy-up north to Gaudí's **Parc Güell** (p20) and, after a relaxing couple of hours, head to Plaça del Sol in Gràcia and let the night take over.

The Catedral's tranquil cloister shows no sign of its resident geese (p15)

Highlights

LA SAGRADA FAMÍLIA (4, G2)

If you have time for only one sight in Barcelona, this emblem of the city, and the project to which Gaudí dedicated most of his working life, should probably be it. It takes up a whole block of l'Eixample, has its own metro station, and is the most talked about and visited unfinished building in the world. After more than 120 years, the church is still only half complete.

INFORMATION

- ☎ 93 207 30 31
- 🖳 www.sagradafa milia.org
- ✉ Carrer de Mallorca 401
- € €8/5 (incl museum), €2 for lift up one of the towers
- 🕒 9am-8pm Apr-Sep, 9am-6pm Oct-Mar
- ℹ bookshop, guided tours (€3, 50mins) up to four times daily
- Ⓜ Sagrada Família
- ♿ fair
- ✕ Alkímia (p78)

An arch-conservative Catholic group dedicated to St Joseph commissioned the building of the Temple Expiatori de la Sagrada Família (Expiatory Temple of the Holy Family) in 1882. Ironically, the work with which Gaudí is most closely associated was not begun by him and will not be completed by him. He replaced another architect in 1884, transformed the plans, and made it his sacred mission for the next 43 years until his death.

He planned three façades, dedicated to the Nativity, Passion and Glory (the main one, on which work is just getting underway). Each is to be crowned by four towers, representing the 12 apostles. Four higher towers will symbolise the Evangelists, while a colossal 170m-high central tower, flanked by another bearing a statue of the Virgin, will represent the Lord.

Only parts of the Nativity façade (facing Carrer de la Marina) were completed in Gaudí's time. He was meticulous about every detail and when asked why he fussed so much about the embellishments on the tops of his towers – which nobody would ever see – he replied, 'the angels will see them'.

From 1912 he devoted all his energies exclusively to what had become his obsession. When funds – and enthusiasm – for the project dried up, he helped by selling all his possessions and took to sleeping on site. No doubt mulling

over some detail of its construction one day in 1926, he was hit by a tram and died in hospital several days later.

In 1936, the year after Gaudí's assistants had completed the Nativity façade, anarchists broke into the workshops and destroyed all the plans and models they could find.

That might have been the end of it, but in the 1940s work was done to repair the damage, and some of Gaudí's models were restored. In 1952 work restarted, and from 1954 to 1976 the Passion façade was raised. Financing comes from private donations from around the world and the ticket takings from the two million or so visitors who stream through each year.

Purists balk at the developments and say Gaudí's unfinished work should have been left intact as a monument to his genius. The use of concrete and inevitable deviations from what are thought to have been Gaudí's plans (rather a moot point, since Gaudí himself tended to make it up as he went along) have raised hackles. The sculptor chosen to decorate the Passion façade, Josep Maria Subirachs, opted for bold lines and stretched images to depict the passion of Christ – an altogether contemporary touch. Work on that façade is now virtually complete. The bulk of the five-nave interior has been roofed over – the ceiling held aloft by a sinewy forest of tree-like pillars. Work on the interior of the apse is underway (the outside was largely done in Gaudí's day) and the first tentative moves to get the Glory façade underway have been made.

Whatever you make of it, you can't help but admire the determination to get the job done. No public money is being spent on the project, but the city is no doubt grateful for its magnetic power over tourists. Speculation on when it might be completed is rife, but no-one expects it to be done before 2026, the centenary of Gaudí's death.

DON'T MISS

- The dream-like ascent to the top of the towers
- Sketches in the museum of how the completed church will look
- The site lit up at night
- A peek into the on-site workshops
- The architect's tomb in the crypt, where you may find a few faithful praying for his beatification

MUSEU PICASSO   (8, B1)

Málaga-born Picasso spent his formative years in Barcelona, knocking about with the young upstarts who helped create Modernisme. He always had a soft spot for the city and in 1962 agreed to assist in the foundation of a museum. His secretary and Barcelona buddy, Jaume Sabartés, donated his private collection, augmented by Picasso and later by his widow.

INFORMATION
- ☎ 93 319 63 10
- 🖥 www.museu picasso.bcn.es
- ✉ Carrer de Montcada 15-23
- € adult/child/ child under 12 €4.80/2.40/free, free 1st Sun of month
- 🕐 10am-8pm Tue-Sat & hols, 10am-3pm Sun
- ⓘ bookshop, guided tours (€3, 50mins) up to four times daily
- Ⓜ Jaume I
- ♿ fair
- ✕ Centre Cultural Euskal Etxea (p75)

Don't just stand there, see something!

The museum is housed in a stunning row of five mostly 14th-century mansions. But be warned: while the collection includes some famous pieces, it is not a showcase for Picasso's most celebrated work. It focuses rather on his early years (until 1904) and provides a unique window on the formation of one of the 20th century's greatest artists.

The collection starts with the teenage Picasso's sketches, oils and doodlings, evidence of his precocious talent. By the latter half of the 1890s he was producing grand portraits inspired by what he was learning in art school – all academic stuff, but remarkable given his young age. From now on he would live away from his parents in various studios around town. The year 1900 was pivotal: he had his first public exhibition in Els Quatre Gats café (p70), got his first taste of Paris and embarked on his first fully self-conscious style experiment, known as the Blue Period.

From here the collection whizzes through the Rose Period and Cubism to settle on his 1950s project to study and redo perspectives of Velázquez's *Las Meninas*. You will also find lithographs, ceramics and engravings. Grand temporary exhibitions are staged frequently.

DON'T MISS
- *Science and Charity* (1897), a realist work Picasso painted in his school years, in which his parents appear as the models
- *El Foll* (The Madman), a disturbing piece from the Blue Period
- The portrait of Senyora Canals, the only item from the Rose Period

MUSEU NACIONAL D'ART DE CATALUNYA (MNAC; 1, B1)

Fans of religious art will be reaching for their rosaries as they contemplate the extraordinary collection of Romanesque art that is the star attraction in the pompous Palau Nacional, built as a temporary pavilion for the World Exhibition in 1929. The remaining collections represent a stroll through the history of mainly Catalan art from Gothic to early-20th-century.

INFORMATION
☎ 93 622 03 75
🖥 www.mnac.es
✉ Miradòr del Palau Nacional
€ adult/student/child under 7 €4.80/3.20/ free, free 1st Thu of month, temporary exhibitions extra
🕓 10am-7pm Tue-Sat, 10am-2.30pm Sun & hols
ℹ bookshop
Ⓜ Espanya
♿ fair

The Romanesque collection consists largely of murals and frescoes from 11th- and 12th-century churches in northern Catalonia. Art historians began salvaging the pieces in the 1920s. The two most striking frescoes are those of Mary and the Christ Child (Room 7), taken from the apse of the church of Santa Maria de Taüll in Catalonia's northwest, and the majestic depiction of Christ (Room 5) from the nearby church of Sant Climent. Some columns bear the illustrative graffiti of monks, bored one afternoon, perhaps 1000 years ago. Frescoes, coins, carvings and altar frontals complement the collection. A frontal (Room 10) depicts bewildered saints being boiled, having nails slammed into their heads and – always a crowd pleaser – being sawn in half from head to toe.

DON'T MISS
- The near perfectly preserved depiction of Christ from the church of Sant Martí de Tosts (Room 3)
- Gothic-era paintings of the martyrdom of St Llúcia and St Vicenç
- Paintings by Modernista leading lights Ramon Casa and Santiago Rusiñol
- Marià Fortuny's realist-era portrait of the Battle of Tetuan

What a shame he can't see inside…

The Gothic art is a broad-ranging mix covering key Catalans such as Bernat Martorell and Jaume Huguet, and art from their contemporaries across Spain. The Cambó collection spans mostly minor works from the 16th century to the 18th century. Catalan artists of the Realist, Modernista and Noucentista movements are featured in the 19th-century rooms. Throw in displays of coins, sketches and engravings, and there you have it.

ESGLÉSIA DE SANTA MARIA DEL MAR (8, B3)

If we make an exception for the extreme oddity of Mr Gaudí's La Sagrada Família church, on which the aesthetics jury will probably remain out for the rest of time, it is true to say that Barcelona's most beautiful and striking church is *not* the Catedral (p15), but this Gothic church dedicated to Our Lady of the Sea in La Ribera.

Built in the 14th century in broad Catalan Gothic style, Santa Maria was lacking in superfluous decoration even before anarchists gutted it in 1909 and, not having had enough, again in 1936.

> **DON'T MISS**
> - The frequent recitals of baroque and classical music held in the evening
> - The plain, stocky octagonal towers flanking the main façade
> - The eight soaring columns, behind the altar, leading your eyes up to the heavens

This only serves to highlight its fine proportions, purity of line and sense of space. Built with, for the time, record-breaking alacrity (in just 59 years – the progress made on La Sagrada Família is positively medieval in comparison), the church is remarkable for its architectural harmony. While many grand European churches portray several styles because they took so long to build, Santa Maria del Mar benefited aesthetically from the haste of its construction. The main body is made up of a central nave and two flanking aisles separated by slender octagonal pillars, creating a sense of enormous lateral space.

> **INFORMATION**
> - ☎ 93 319 05 16
> - ✉ Plaça de Santa Maria del Mar
> - € free
> - ☯ 9am-1.30pm & 4.30-8pm daily
> - Ⓜ Jaume I
> - ✖ L'Ou Com Balla (p77)

Just opposite the southern flank of the church an eternal flame burns brightly over an apparently anonymous sunken square. This was once **El Fossar de les Moreres** (the Mulberry Cemetery), where Catalan resistance fighters were buried after the siege of Barcelona ended in defeat in September 1714. The cemetery's name derived from the mulberry trees that once grew here, but nowadays all that remain are the name and the flame.

MUSEU D'HISTÒRIA DE LA CIUTAT (3, C3)

The entrance to this museum is through 16th-century mansion Casa Padellàs, shifted here in the 1930s to make way for the bustling ramrod artery Via Laietana. Digging the foundations one day, what should labourers stub their shovels on but the ancient Roman city of Barcino!

So, with a chance beginning, this remarkable and superbly presented museum – with the largest underground excavation of any ancient city in Europe – was born. Stroll through the town along glass ramps and peer down at the wheel ruts gouged into roads two millennia ago. Explore public baths, drainage systems and a mosaic on the porch of a house.

Peer into storage areas for wine and *garum* (a whiffy fish sauce popular throughout the Roman empire). They reckon that, if you concentrate hard enough, you can still smell the pungent export. You walk along part of the city wall and can inspect a couple of towers. Around 4500 sq metres have been excavated, extending beneath Plaça del Rei and to the Catedral, where you can see a Visigothic baptismal font.

INFORMATION
- ☎ 93 315 11 11
- 🖥 www.museu historia.bcn.es
- ✉ Carrer del Veguer
- € €4/2.50 (includes access to Museu-Monestir de Pedralbes), free 4-8pm 1st Sat of month, temporary exhibitions €3.50/1.50
- 🕐 10am-2pm & 4-8pm Tue-Sat, 10am-3pm Sun Oct-May, 10am-8pm Tue-Sat, 10am-3pm Sun Jun-Sep
- Ⓜ Jaume I
- ✖ Comme-Bio (p76)

DON'T MISS
- Capella Reial de Santa Àgata, the 14th-century royal chapel
- The 15th-century altarpiece by Jaume Huguet in Capella Reial de Santa Àgata
- Traces of the Romanesque predecessor to the Catedral

Ancient Barcino – fishy

After Barcino, you emerge into buildings of the former royal palace and can admire the broad arches of the **Saló del Tinell**, a 14th-century banquet hall where Columbus breathlessly told King Fernando and Queen Isabel of his discovery of the western route to 'India' (close, but no cigar).

Climb up inside the oddly stout 16th-century tower known as the **Mirador del Rei Martí** (lookout tower of King Martin) for splendid views of medieval Barcelona.

L'AQUÀRIUM (4, H5)

This is about as close as you'll come to saying 'how do you do' to a shark without donning a wetsuit or having an unexpected encounter off a tropical beach somewhere. The 80m-long shark tunnel is doubtless the high point of a visit here.

INFORMATION
- ☎ 93 221 74 74
- 🖥 www.aquarium bcn.com
- ✉ Maremàgnum, Port Vell
- € €13.50/9.25
- 🕙 9.30am-9pm Mon-Fri, 9am-9.30pm Sat & Sun Oct-May, 9.30am-9.30pm daily Jun & Sep, 9am-11pm daily Jul & Aug
- ℹ bookshop, special activities
- Ⓜ Drassanes
- ✕ cafeteria-restaurant
- ♿ good

Eye to eye with an untroubled occupant

The aquarium (one of the largest in Europe) has the world's best Mediterranean collection and is divided into 21 tanks. Some 8000 fish (including about a dozen sharks) have become permanent residents here in an area filled with 4.5 million litres of water.

The restless sharks in the eponymous tunnel are not alone. A band of other deep sea critters, from splendid flapping rays to huge sunfish, float about here, seemingly undisturbed by their formidable playmates. As you proceed, the sharks will glide above you, allowing a frighteningly full view of their endless rows of teeth.

But there is much more. One tank is devoted exclusively to the delights of the Red Sea, a multicoloured affair teeming with butterfly fish, angelfish and surgeon fish, just to name a few. The Caribbean, Hawaiian, Australian and South Seas tanks provide a similar festival of submarine colour.

The serious sea-critter observer may have more interest in the less flamboyant display devoted to Mediterranean sea life (yes, there's still some left!), the aquarium's speciality. Across a series of tanks you will see moray eels, bream and red mullet, mixed in with cute little seahorses and other creatures from a variety of Med environments.

DON'T MISS
- The interactive Planeta Agua zone with, among other beasties, a family of Antarctic penguins
- Patting the stingrays in a supervised tank in the Planeta Agua area
- The ugly rockfish, scorpion fish and other deep-sea dangerous fellows all together in one happy tank
- The South American piranhas, safely behind glass

CATEDRAL (3, B2)

Soaring above the Barri Gòtic, Barcelona's central place of worship presents a magnificent image. It is a towering monument to more than 1500 years of continuous Catalan worship and the third church to be built on what was once the northern half of the Roman town.

The imposing, decorative façade was only added in the late 19th century (albeit to a 15th-century late-Gothic design), while the rest was built from 1298 to 1460. The interior is immense, divided into a central nave and two aisles by lines of slim, elegant pillars. One of the few churches spared the arson attacks of anarchists during the Civil War, it retains its ornamentation intact.

Inside the main entrance to your left is a baptistry, where the six Native Americans brought back by Columbus in 1493 as souvenirs and proof of his discoveries were allegedly baptised. Smack in the middle of the central nave are the 14th-century sculpted **choir stalls** (€1.50), which face the **crypt** of Santa Eulàlia, one of Barcelona's two patron saints. Along the wall past the southwest transept are the coffins of Count Ramon Berenguer I and his wife, Almodis, founders of the Catedral's 11th-century Romanesque predecessor.

INFORMATION
- ☎ 93 315 15 54
- ✉ Plaça de la Seu
- € Catedral free; choir stalls, chapter house & roof €2 each; special visit (see below) €4
- 🕐 8am-1.15pm & 5-7.30pm, special visit 1.30-5pm. In the morning or afternoon, entrance to the Catedral itself is free, and you can opt to visit any combination of the choir stalls, chapter house and roof. The special visit includes admission to the Catedral, choir stalls, chapter house and roof, and is less crowded.
- Ⓜ Jaume I
- ♿ fair
- ✕ Shunka (p72)

DON'T MISS
- Sant Crist de Lepant, the crucifix borne into the Battle of Lepanto by Don Juan's flagship in 1571 – they say it dodged a Turkish cannon ball
- The Romanesque chapel of Santa Llúcia
- The alabaster tomb of Santa Eulàlia, decorated by Pisan sculptors
- A trip to the roof for a pigeon's-eye view of the city

Through a Romanesque door (the only surviving remnant from the Romanesque church) you can head out into the lovely, shady **cloister**. The chaplains have kept honking geese here around the fountain from time immemorial. Just why is another matter, but the geese make fine watchdogs! Off the cloister is the **Sala Capitular** (chapter house, €1.50), which contains a handful of religious paintings.

LA PEDRERA (6, B3)

The most extraordinary apartment block ever built in Barcelona was originally called Casa Milà – after its owner – but was nicknamed La Pedrera

INFORMATION
- ☎ 902 400973
- 🖥 www.caixa catalunya.es
- ✉ Carrer de Provença 261-265
- € €7/3.50
- 🕙 10am-8pm
- ℹ shop, temporary exhibitions held, guided tours in English 4pm daily
- Ⓜ Diagonal
- ♿ good
- ✕ Tragaluz (p79)

(The Stone Quarry) by the bemused locals who watched Antoni Gaudí build it from 1905 to 1910. Its rippling grey stone façade looks more like a cliff face sculpted by waves and wind than something made by human hands, and is studded with 'seaweed' in the form of wrought-iron balconies.

On the fourth floor you can visit a recreated Modernista apartment, **El Pis de la Pedrera**, furnished in the style a prosperous family might have enjoyed when the block was completed. No two apartments are the same, but this one – with its sensuous curves and stylish little touches – is filled with antiques from the era and makes for a fascinating wander.

The **Espai Gaudí** (Gaudí Space) is housed in what used to be the attic and feels like the building's ribcage. It now offers a thorough overview of Gaudí's work and methods, and screens a wonderful visual display of many of Gaudí's other key works, including some outside Barcelona.

Upstairs is the **roof**, adorned with what look like giant medieval (or 21st-century!) knights but are in fact the most photographed chimneypots in the world. Gaudí, a firmly religious fellow, wanted to erect a 12m statue of the Virgin up here and when Milà refused (anticlerical anarchists had rampaged through the city in riots in 1909), he resigned from the project, vowing never to work for the bourgeoisie again.

DON'T MISS
- Rooftop *cava* (Spanish sparkling wine) and concerts on Friday and Saturday nights in summer (€10)
- The extraordinary parabolic arches of the attic
- The views from the roof and El Pis de la Pedrera

CASA BATLLÒ (6, B4)

Yes, La Pedrera does have competition, across the road and just a few blocks away…and lo! It's by the same guy! Here Gaudí completed probably the most striking renovation project in Barcelona just before moving on to build La Pedrera.

DON'T MISS
- The old-fashioned lift in the centre of the building
- The laser light show on Gaudí's design curves
- The views from the roof

Just keeping up with the Joneses…

Casa Batlló is one of three buildings done by leading lights of the Modernista movement and collectively known as the **Manzana de la Discordia** (p39), but it is right out there on its own. Best of all, since 2002 it has been open to the public, and the queues show that it has been a brilliant success with visitors to Barcelona.

The façade, sprinkled with bits of blue, mauve and green tile, and studded with wave-shaped window frames and balconies, rises to an uneven blue-tiled roof with a solitary tower. Locals know it as the *casa dels ossos* (house of bones) or *casa del drac* (house of the dragon).

When Gaudí was commissioned to refashion this building, he went to town inside and out. The internal light patios shimmer with tiles of deep sea-blue. The staircase wafts you up to the first floor. The main salon, looking on to Passeig de Gràcia, is a twisting whirl. Everything from the doors to the ceiling design is a festival of bends and curves.

The same themes continue in the other rooms and covered terrace. As you walk out onto the latter, the floor on either side is obscurely transparent and shot with more curvaceous motifs. In March 2004 the incredible roof with its twisting tiled chimneys was also opened to the public, officially as a temporary arrangement, but then that was the story when they opened the building in 2002!

INFORMATION
- ☎ 93 216 03 06
- 🖳 www.casabatllo.es, in Castilian
- ✉ Passeig de Gràcia 43
- € €10, €16 incl roof
- 🕙 9am-2pm Mon-Sat, 9am-8pm Sun
- ⓘ audio guides available
- Ⓜ Passeig de Gràcia
- ♿ fair
- ✗ Cerveseria Catalana (p78)

FUNDACIÓ JOAN MIRÓ (1, B1)

Forever leaving a piece of himself in his native Barcelona, Joan Miró established this gallery on the hill of Montjuïc in 1971. The largest single collection of his work is housed here, in a magnificent building designed by his friend Josep Lluís Sert. The combination of natural light, white walls and airy galleries make this a wonderful setting to appreciate the works of Catalonia's greatest artist.

INFORMATION
- ☎ 93 443 94 70
- 🖥 www.bcn.fjmiro.es
- ✉ Plaça de Neptu
- € €7.20/3.90, temp exhibitions €3.60/1.80
- 🕐 10am-7pm Tue, Wed, Fri & Sat, 10am-9.30pm Thu, 10am-2.30pm Sun & hols
- ℹ book & art shop, contemporary art library, audio guide available
- 🚌 50, 55, 61 & PM
- ♿ good
- ✕ restaurant-café

Miró, although principally a painter, dabbled in every medium he could get his hands on, and the museum houses sculptures, engravings, lithographs and ceramics, a huge legacy of drawings and other work, and more than 300 paintings. Only a small part of the collection can be displayed at any time, but still there is always far too much to take in on just one visit.

The permanent exhibition tends to concentrate on Miró's more settled final years, but it also gives captivating insights into the evolution of his work and traces the changes in his style and his rebellion against conventional painting. Many of the works reflect his trademark delicate, yet aggressive, use of primary colours and symbols, while others convey his wit and sense of the absurd. There are also many wonderful sculptures in and around the building, by Miró and others, and one room contains paintings donated by other artists after Miró's death in 1983.

The foundation is much more than a place to house Miró's work, however – it hosts impressive temporary shows, has a good library and occasionally stages concerts.

DON'T MISS
- Alexander Calder's *Mercury Fountain* (1937)
- Miró's *Man and Woman in Front of a Pile of Excrement* (1935)
- Sculptures on the terrace
- The Miró papers, including sketches and preparatory drawings

I'll take it – can you giftwrap it?

LA RAMBLA (5, D2)

Spain's most famous street is the main artery of old Barcelona and where visitors inevitably head upon arrival. Flanked by narrow traffic lanes, it is a broad, tree-lined pedestrian boulevard, crowded from dusk till dusk with a constant flow of locals and *guiris* (out-of-towners).

It may not be typical of Barcelona, but it's the city's most extroverted side; a stage for an assortment of street performers, from flamenco dancers to fire-eaters and more human statues than you could possibly knock over in one go. It's dotted with overpriced pavement cafés and restaurants that nevertheless provide the perfect spot from which to take the city's pulse as you watch the humanity saunter past.

INFORMATION
Ⓜ Catalunya, Liceu, Drassanes
Ⓧ Bar Kasparo (p73)

There's never a dull moment on La Rambla, whether your funny bone is being tickled or your pocket picked. Prostitutes (of all persuasions) work the lower half of the strip, and in between the bird, flower and news stalls you will always find the occasional three-card trickster.

La Rambla gets its name from a seasonal stream (*raml* in Arabic) that ran here. It became a clogged sewer by the 14th century and was filled in by the 18th-century, when trees were planted and mansions built. It changes name five times along its 1.25km way, which is why you may hear it called Las Ramblas. At the top, La Rambla de Canaletes is named after the century-old fountain that dispenses the purest water in the city. If you drink from it, locals say, you will return to Barcelona – worse things could happen!

DON'T MISS
- A cocktail at Boadas (p84)
- A wander around La Boqueria market (p63)
- Chocolates from Escribà (p58)
- Mosaïc de Miró (p37) in Plaça del la Boqueria

PARC GÜELL (4, E1)

The place where Gaudí turned his hand to landscape gardening is one of the most wonderful on the planet – a jovial and enchanting spot to relax, unwind and rub shoulders with the locals. It's not a sight to visit and tick off your list. It's a minor hassle to get here and can only be fully appreciated if you've got time up your sleeve and relaxation on your mind.

INFORMATION
- ☎ 93 413 24 00
- ✉ Carrer d'Olot 7
- € park free
- ☾ 9am-9pm Jun-Sep, 9am-8pm Apr, May & Oct, 9am-7pm Mar & Nov, 10am-6pm Dec-Feb
- ⓘ Centre d'Interpretació i Acollida (below)
- Ⓜ Lesseps (and a steep signposted walk)
- 🚌 No 24

The park originated in 1900, when Gaudí's patron, Eusebi Güell, commissioned him to create a garden suburb for the hoity-toity on a hill overlooking the city. The venture, a monumental commercial flop, was abandoned in 1914. But by then Gaudí, in his inimitable style, had created a unique space where the artificial almost seems more natural than the endeavours of Mother Nature.

The lavishly ceramic-decorated entrance – guarded by a mosaic serpent, a favourite emblem of the city – is flanked by two fairytale-style houses. Another, off to your right, houses the Casa Museu Gaudí (p27). The steps lead to the **Sala Hipóstila**, a forest of 86 stone columns, originally intended to form a covered market. To the left, a gallery with twisted stonework columns gives the impression of a cloister beneath tree roots – a motif repeated throughout the park.

Above is a wonderful esplanade, whose focal point is the **Banc de Trencadís**, a delightful bench that snakes playfully around its perimeter and is clad with candy-coloured ceramics (designed by Gaudí's assistant and architect Josep Maria Jujol).

Beyond lie 3km of roads, walks and porticos that wind their way around the wooded hill, affording spectacular views of the city.

A Gingerbread House
Just inside the park entrance from Carrer d'Olot, the Pavelló de Conser-geria (one of the fairytale houses and the former porter's lodge) nowadays houses the **Centre d'Interpretació i Acollida** (☎ 93 285 68 99; adult/student/child under 16 €2/1.50/free; ☾ 11am-3pm), a display dedicated to Gaudí's unique building methods.

MUSEU DEL FUTBOL CLUB BARCELONA (4, B5)

For many people, Football Club Barcelona is the embodiment of the Catalan spirit. One of Europe's biggest (and wealthiest) clubs, it is magnificently housed in the Camp Nou stadium, which is one of the world's largest football arenas. Although it tends to run second to archrival Real Madrid, this club can't be beaten for colour, character, big names and passion.

Founded in 1899, it has been in the highest echelon of Spanish football ever since. Despite the Catalan nationalist rhetoric, its links with foreigners have been strong and in recent years the team has largely comprised outrageously well-paid foreign mercenaries.

If you can't get to a match (see p94), the Museu del Futbol Club Barcelona will provide some consolation (and a view of the stadium). It's a busy spot and normally as crowded as the six-yard box for a corner. The crowds are made up of football fanatics, tolerant partners and coachloads of package tourists who just heard it was popular. Despite the volume of people, it maintains the hushed reverence of a cathedral.

Dragged-along partners may find it surprisingly charming – perhaps more so than the dragging fanatics. On display are stacks of old photographs, mementos, models, sculptures, posters, programmes, jerseys, boots and balls. Pride of place in the trophy cabinet is the 1992 European Cup. To be honest, though, when it's not your own team, it can get a bit ho-hum.

Downstairs there's a huge store selling Barcelona merchandise, the highlight of which is an enormously tacky stall that will provide a photograph of you wearing the Barça colours and scoring a goal in Camp Nou stadium.

INFORMATION
☎ 93 496 36 08
🖳 www.fcbarcelona.es
✉ Carrer d'Aristides Maillol
€ €5.30/3.70
☼ 10am-6.30pm Mon-Sat, 10am-2pm Sun & hols
ⓘ guided tours of the museum and stadium (€9.50/6.60; 10am-5.30pm Mon-Sat, 10am-1pm Sun & hols)
Ⓜ Collblanc
♿ good
🍴 café

Bums for Barça

Football Club Barcelona is a big club with a huge fan base – in 2004 there were 112,000 offical members, and the number was rising. The *culers* (bums), as the fans are affectionately known, got the delightful nickname from people who used to pass the stadium when matches were on and see rows of posteriors hanging over the perimeter wall.

MUSEU MARÍTIM (5, C6)

To appreciate where much of Barcelona's medieval splendour came from, you need to visit this museum, which recounts the seafaring history of what was for centuries one of the most bustling mercantile cities in the Mediterranean.

INFORMATION
- ☎ 93 342 99 20
- 🖥 www.diba.es /mmaritim
- ✉ Avinguda de les Drassanes
- € €5.40/2.70
- ⏰ 10am-7pm
- Ⓜ Drassanes
- ♿ good
- ✗ restaurant-café

Captain, we seem to have run aground…

The Reials Drassanes (Royal Shipyards), completed in 1378, are a superb example of civic Catalan Gothic architecture. Up to 30 galleys could be built beneath their lofty arches at any one time and then slipped directly into the Mediterranean, which lapped the seaward side of the buildings until the 18th century. By then, there was no need to build ships here any more, and the yards were neglected until the 1980s, when one of the city's most captivating exhibitions, the Museu Marítim, was installed.

The highlight is a life-size replica of Don Juan of Austria's flagship **galley**, which he successfully took into batt le against the Turks off Lepanto in 1571, the last great sea struggle between fleets of galleys, and a famous (if inconclusive) victory for Christianity.

This battle, the history of maritime Barcelona and lots of kid-friendly adventures are presented in a series of simulations with headphone commentaries provided in English. Among the extensive collection of maritime paraphernalia are vessels of all types and epochs, from coastal fishing skips to giants of the steam age. Other displays include models of the vessels Columbus led on his first voyage of accidental discovery of the Americas in 1492.

Outside the museum, alongside the Moll de la Fusta, you can board the **Pailebot Santa Eulàlia**, a 46m-long timber sailing ship from 1918.

DON'T MISS
- Abraham i Jafuda Cresque's 1375 map of the known world
- Captains' logs, navigation charts and models of ships from the age of steam
- Plumbing the (simulated) depths with one of the world's first submariners, Catalan Narcis Monturiol i Estarriol
- Life-size diorama remakes of Barcelona docklands

MUSEU-MONESTIR DE PEDRALBES (4, A3)

This uniquely peaceful corner of Barcelona provides an absorbing insight into medieval monastic life. An additional attraction since 1993 has been a chunk of the Thyssen-Bornemisza Collection (Col.lecció Thyssen-Bornemisza) of paintings from the 13th century to the 17th century (the rest of them are in Madrid). This collection is, however, destined eventually to be moved to the Museu Nacional d'Art de Catalunya (p11).

INFORMATION
- ☎ 93 203 92 82
- 🖳 www.museu historia.bcn.es
- ✉ Baixada del Monestir 9
- € €5.50, or €4 for the monastery alone, which includes Museu d'Història de la Ciutat
- 🕑 10am-2pm Tue-Sun
- 🚃 FGC Reina Elisenda
- 🚌 Nos 22, 64 & 75

The site features a convent founded in 1326 – quickly built but scarcely touched since. It is considered a jewel of Catalan Gothic architecture and contains a lovely three-storey cloister with a fountain and landscaped garden. It still functions as a convent, sheltering a small group of Poor Clare sisters, whom you can sometimes espy shuffling behind grills erected to partition their closed quarters.

DON'T MISS
- Fra Angelico's magnificent *Madonna of Humility* in the Thyssen-Bornemisza Collection
- Murals by Ferrer Bassá (1346) in the Capella de Sant Miquel
- The simple Catalan Gothic church alongside the convent

As you head around the cloister you can inspect the trappings of convent life and visit the restored refectory, kitchen, stables, stores and infirmary. The latter houses a stunningly intricate series of dioramas on the life of Christ by Joan Mari. Built into the cloister walls are preserved day cells where the nuns spent most of their time in prayer and devotional reading.

The Thyssen-Bornemisza Collection is located in the spectacularly renovated nuns' dormitory. The 70 religious paintings include works from European masters such as Canaletto, Rubens, Tintoretto, Titian, Zurbarán and Velázquez. There are also works from the Renaissance period in Germany, some late-baroque paintings and a collection of sculptures by anonymous medieval Italian artists.

PALAU DE LA MÚSICA CATALANA (5, F1)

Come for a concert at the Palace of Catalan Music and you risk being distracted from the performance by the richness of the setting. A symbolic home to Catalan nationalist sentiment, it's one of the crown jewels of Barcelona Modernisme.

At the beginning of the 20th century, the Orfeó Català musical society asked Domènech i Montaner to build a temple to the Catalan Renaixença (Renaissance). The brief fired his enthusiasm, and he gathered the best Catalan artisans of the age to help him. But, unpaid and cheesed off, Montaner didn't attend the opening in 1908 when his masterpiece was unveiled.

INFORMATION

- ☎ 93 295 72 00
- ▯ www.palaumusica
  .org
- ✉ Carrer de Sant
  Francesc de Paula 2
- € adult/student/child
  under 12 €8/7/free
  by guided tour
- ☽ 50-minute tours
  every half-hour
  10am-3.30pm
- Ⓜ Urquinaona
- ♿ good
- ✗ Els Quatre Gats
  (p70)

The palace's bare-brick façade of mosaics, tile-clad pillars and busts only hints at the profound splendour within. Montaner considered the building 'the garden of music', and decoration blooms everywhere, among ornate busts and sculptures that pay euphoric tribute to Catalan music and the music Catalans love.

DON'T MISS

- 'Forest' balcony, with 14 different pillar trees
- A show, any show
- Medieval-style chandeliers

But all this pales in comparison to the auditorium, a staggering symphony of ceramics and stained glass with room for 2000 spectators. Flanking the stage are a bust of Beethoven, a towering sculpture of Wagner's Valkyries, Josep Anselm Clavé (founder of the Orfeó), and a medley of maidens. Muses, half ceramic and half sculpture, burst from the back wall raring to join in the performance. By day, light streams in from a spectacular skylight, the centrepiece of the chamber. Since 1989, work has been done to modernise the concert facilities and, from 2000, add new performance space.

Do you do weddings?

PARC DE LA CIUTADELLA (5, J3)

For a snooze in the green, the Parc de la Ciutadella could be for you. You'd never know that, until the demolition order came through in 1869, a menacing fortress aimed at controlling the locals had occupied most of this area for over a century. Felipe V razed a populous city quarter and built La Ciutadella (the citadel) after taking Barcelona at the end of the War of the Spanish Succession in 1714. The area became the main site for the Universal Exhibition of 1888, and thereafter a park.

DON'T MISS
- Rowing a boat on the artificial lake
- Checking out the Zoo de Barcelona (p44)
- Antoni Tàpies' odd *Homenatge a Picasso* sculpture on Passeig de Picasso
- The statue of a woolly mammoth near the Cascada

The Cascada: a mammoth's natural habitat

The single most impressive sight in the park is the monumental **Cascada** (waterfall) created in 1875–81 by Josep Fontsère with the help of a young Gaudí. It's a dramatic combination of classical statuary, rugged rocks, greenery and thundering water.

Southeast, in the fort's former arsenal, is the **Parlament de Catalunya** (☎ 93 304 65 00; free guided visits for groups by appointment; ☾ 9am-2pm & 4-8pm Mon-Fri), where the regional parliament sits.

Of the buildings on the Passeig de Picasso side of the park, the **Castell dels Tres Dragons** is the most curious and now houses the **Museu de Zoologia** (p29). To the south is **L'Hivernacle**, one of two arboretums, a mini botanical garden with a pleasant café. Next is the **Museu de Geologia** (p29). Further along from the museum is **L'Umbracle**, another arboretum.

Northwest of the park, Passeig de Lluís Companys is capped by the Islamic-style brickwork, Modernista **Arc de Triomf** (p38), raised as an entrance to the Universal Exhibition.

PALAU GÜELL   (5, C4)

This mansion – one of the few Modernista buildings in the old town – is just a hop and a skip from La Rambla. It was Antoni Gaudí's first major work, built in the late 1880s for his patron, Eusebi Güell. Although somewhat muted by the flamboyant genius's standards, it's still a riot of different styles and materials (considered unworthy by the establishment of the time).

INFORMATION
- ☎ 93 317 39 74
- ✉ Carrer Nou de la Rambla 3-5
- € €3/1.50
- ⏱ 10am-6.15pm Mon-Sat Jun-Sep, 10am-4.15pm Oct-Apr
- Ⓜ Drassanes
- ✗ Organic (p75)

The compulsory guided tour starts in the subterranean stables (with fanning bare-brick pillars and arches), where police tortured political prisoners after the Civil War. Dark-grey marble stairs lead to the first floor and a series of vestibules with columned galleries overhanging the street, designed to maximise space and natural light. The decoration becomes more ornate, and the original Modernista furniture more sumptuous, as you near the heart of the house – the salon. Functions and gatherings took place in this impressive room, where the walls stretch up three floors to form a dome. What remains of the family chapel is reached through 5m panels made of hardwoods and ivory, and sheathed in horn and tortoiseshell. The family apartments are on the next floor.

While the place is a masterfully crafted insight into Modernisme, the effect is on the sombre side. But all is forgiven when you emerge onto the rippled roof, a remarkable forest of unique chimney sculptures clad in colourful mosaics. From here you can peer over to a studio at No 6 where Picasso, who loathed Gaudí's work, began his Blue Period in 1902.

DON'T MISS
- The Modernista furniture, which the tour passes over
- The spyholes in the visitors' gallery (through which Güell eavesdropped on guests)
- The spiral walkway to the basement, designed to accommodate horse-drawn coaches

The start of something beautiful? Ask Picasso...

Sights & Activities

MUSEUMS & GALLERIES

CaixaForum (1, A1)

Housed in a former Modernista factory designed by Josep Puig i Cadafalch, this extensive private collection of contemporary art is in constant flux. The Caixa building society rotates its international line-up of works and organises frequent temporary exhibitions, which means that no two visits will be the same. Among the names in the permanent collection are such Spanish icons as Antoni Tàpies and Miquel Barceló. In the courtyard is a steel tree designed by Japanese architect Arata Isozaki.

☎ 93 476 86 00
✉ Avinguda del Marquès de Comillas 6-8, Montjuïc
€ free ☾ 10am-8pm Tue-Sun Ⓜ Espanya
♿ good

Casa Museu Gaudí (4, E1)

Worth a gander if you're in Parc Güell (p20), this is the house where Gaudí spent many of his later years. The museum includes remarkable Modernista furniture, designed by Gaudí and his mates, along with personal effects and an ascetically narrow bed upon which he probably fantasised about completing La Sagrada Família.

☎ 93 219 38 11
✉ Parc Güell, Carrer d'Olot 7, Zona Alta € €4
☾ 10am-8pm Apr-Sep, 10am-6pm Oct-Mar
Ⓜ Lesseps (then walk following signs) 🚌 24

Centre de Cultura Contemporània de Barcelona (CCCB; 5, B1)

Loved by locals, this multiuse cultural centre has a dynamic atmosphere. It occupies the shell of an 18th-century hospice and hosts a constantly changing programme of exhibitions on urban design, 20th-century arts, architecture and the city itself. It also organises and hosts dance performances, lectures and forums.

☎ 93 306 41 00
✉ Carrer de Montalegre 5, El Raval € €4/3
☾ 11am-8pm Tue-Sat, 11am-3pm Sun & hols 21 Jun–21 Sep, 11am-2pm & 4-8pm Tue, Thu & Fri, 11am-8pm Wed & Sat, 11am-7pm Sun & hols 22 Sep-20 Jun Ⓜ Universitat ♿ good

Fundació Antoni Tàpies (6, B4)

This Domènech i Montaner building – considered by many to be the prototype for Modernisme, and the first in the city to be built on an iron frame – houses the experimental work of Catalonia's greatest living artist, Antoni Tàpies, as well as exhibitions by other contemporary artists. The building is crowned with coiled wire, a Tàpies sculpture titled *Núvol i Cadira* (Cloud and Chair),

See stars at CaixaForum

which looks curious by day and spectacular by night.
☎ 93 487 03 15
🖳 www.fundaciotapies.org ✉ Carrer d'Aragó 255, L'Eixample
€ €4.20/2.10 🕑 10am-8pm Tue-Sun Ⓜ Passeig de Gràcia ♿ good

Fundación Francisco Godia (6, C4) An intriguing mix of medieval art, ceramics and modern paintings makes up this eclectic private collection. Medieval works include wooden sculptures of the Virgin Mary and Christ taken down from the Cross, and there are paintings by such Catalan icons as Jaume Huguet and Valencia's Joaquim Sorolla.
☎ 93 272 31 80 🖳 www.fundacionfgodia.org ✉ Carrer de València 284, L'Eixample € €4.20/2.10 🕑 10am-8pm Wed-Mon Ⓜ Passeig de Gràcia ♿ good

Galería Maeght (8, B2) After the crowds of the nearby Museu Picasso, it's a calming and sensuous treat to walk around this gallery, which occupies a beautiful 16th-century mansion. The local branch of the prestigious Paris-based outfit, it showcases the work of established painters and sculptors from around Europe.
☎ 93 310 42 45 🖳 www.maeght.com, in French ✉ Carrer de Montcada 25, La Ribera € free 🕑 10am-2pm & 4-8pm Tue-Sat Ⓜ Jaume I ♿ fair

Galería Olímpica (1, B2) A museum chock-full of photographs and memo-

Art flourishes at the Fundació Antoni Tàpies

rabilia associated with the 1992 Barcelona Olympics – one for dedicated anoraks. Favourite items are the scrumptious-looking models of the standard daily diet (baked beans anyone?) of cyclists and gymnasts. A whole display is dedicated to Cobi, the 1992 Olympic Games mascot dreamed up by the ubiquitous Valencian designer Javier Mariscal.
☎ 93 426 06 60 🖳 www.fundaciobarcelonaolimpica.es ✉ Passeig Olímpic s/n, Montjuïc € €2.50 🕑 10am-1pm & 4-6pm Mon-Fri 🚌 50, 61 & PM ♿ fair

Museu Barbier-Mueller d'Art Precolombí (8, B1) In this branch of the prestigious Barbier-Mueller museum in Geneva you'll find a sparkling assortment of art from the pre-Columbian civilisations of Central and South America. Exquisite gold jewellery forms the introduction, followed by a series of rooms containing ceramics, jewellery, textiles and other objects.
☎ 93 310 45 16 🖳 www.barbier-mueller.ch

✉ Carrer de Montcada 12-14, La Ribera € adult/student/child under 16 €3/1.50/free, free 1st Sun of month 🕑 10am-6pm Tue-Sat, 10am-3pm Sun & hols Ⓜ Jaume I ♿ fair

Museu d'Arqueologia de Catalunya (1, B1) This archaeology museum mainly features artefacts discovered in Catalonia and Mediterranean Spain, ranging from copies of pre-Neanderthal skulls to jewel-studded Visigoth crosses. It also features a statue of a splendidly endowed, and routinely aroused, Priapus (the God of male procreative power) that we're not allowed to inspect closely.
☎ 93 424 65 77 🖳 www.mac.es ✉ Passeig de Santa Madrona 39-41, Montjuïc € €2.40/1.70 🕑 9.30am-7pm Tue-Sat, 10am-2.30pm Sun 🚌 55 & PM ♿ good

Museu d'Art Contemporani de Barcelona (MACBA; 5, B2) This gleaming, glassy structure was dropped on El Raval in 1995 and, after a few years finding its way, now shines as a stage for the best of Catalan, Spanish and international contemporary art. Works start with artists such as Antoni Tàpies, Joan Brossa, Paul Klee, Alexander Calder and Miquel Barceló, but the display is in constant, restless flux. The gallery also presents temporary exhibitions.

☎ 93 412 08 10 ▯ www .macba.es ✉ Plaça dels Àngels 1, El Raval € €7/5.50 🕑 11am-7.30pm Mon, Wed, Thu & Fri, 10am-8pm Sat, 10am-3pm Sun & hols, longer hrs summer Ⓜ Universitat ♿ good

Museu de Ceràmica (4, B4)

This attractive museum has perhaps the most fragile exhibits in Barcelona: an exceptional collection of Spanish ceramics from medieval times to the present day. It includes some pieces by Miró and Picasso, as well as a charming section of tiles depicting Catalan life.

☎ 93 280 50 24 ▯ www .museuceramica.bcn.es ✉ Palau Reial de Pedralbes, Avinguda Diagonal 686, Zona Alta € €3.50/2 (incl Museu de les Arts Decoratives & Museu Tèxtil i d'Indumentàra), free 1st Sun of month 🕑 10am-6pm Tue-Sat, 10am-3pm Sun & hols Ⓜ Palau Reial ♿ good

Museu de Geologia (5, H3)

If geology doesn't grab you, neither will this vast collection of minerals, rocks and fossils in the city's oldest municipal museum.

☎ 93 319 68 95 ✉ Passeig de Picasso, Parc de la Ciutadella € €3 (incl Museu de Zoologia) 🕑 10am-2pm Tue, Wed & Fri-Sun, 10am-6.30pm Thu Ⓜ Arc de Triomf

Museu de les Arts Decoratives (4, B4)

Occupying the same former palace as the Museu de Ceràmica (see left), this series of galleries overlooks a stunningly sumptuous oval

throne room and features a collection of furniture and decorative objects from the early Middle Ages to the kitsch 1970s.

☎ 93 280 50 24 ▯ www .museuartsdecoratives .bcn.es ✉ Palau Reial de Pedralbes, Avinguda Diagonal 686, Zona Alta € €3.50/2 (incl Museu de Ceràmica & Museu Tèxtil i d'Indumentàra), free 1st Sun of month 🕑 10am-6pm Tue-Sat, 10am-3pm Sun & hols Ⓜ Palau Reial ♿ good

Museu de Zoologia (Castell dels Tres Dragons; 5, H3)

This rather fusty old institution is the place for stuffed animals, model elephants and skeletons of huge things that lived in the past. What makes it interesting is the building itself – a whimsical construction by Domènech i Montaner, who adorned his 'castle' with fantasy ceramic coats of arms.

☎ 93 319 69 12 ✉ Passeig de Picasso,

Come to the Mountain

Montjuïc, possibly meaning 'Jewish mount' (centuries-old Jewish tombstones have been unearthed here), makes for a rich couple of days' exploration. People come for culture at the Fundació Joan Miró (p18), CaixaForum (p27) and Museu Nacional d'Art de Catalunya (p11), and a host of other sights, including the 1992 Olympic Games installations, Castell de Montjuïc, minor museums, the many gardens, swimming pools and more.

Grab the **Montjuïc Card** (€20/10). Valid for a day (not issued on Monday), the card gets you entry to all the attractions, as well as transport options including a circle-line tourist train, the Telefèric de Montjuïc cable car and use of hire bicycles available at key points around the mountain.

The card is available from the **park information office** (1, B1; ☎ 93 289 28 30; Passeig de Santa Madrona 28; 🕑 10am-6pm) in the Font del Gat building, at the bicycle-rental points and at tourist offices.

Rolling with the Crowds

You can't fully appreciate the subtlety of Miró or the genius of Gaudí when you're standing on your tiptoes looking over somebody else's shoulder. Unfortunately, there's no sure way of beating the crowds, and queues form at the most popular sights before the box office even opens. La Sagrada Família is at its best in the early evening when the coach tours retire to buffet, the Museu Picasso settles down around lunchtime and Miró looks his best in the morning. The crowds generally surge and recede at the busiest places, so if the numbers are getting you down just retire to the café and wait. When the café fills up, it's a good time to see the sight.

Parc de la Ciutadella
€ €3 (incl Museu de Geologia) ⏰ 10am-2pm Tue, Wed & Fri-Sun, 10am-6.30pm Thu
Ⓜ Arc de Triomf ♿ good

Museu del Perfum (6, B4)
A thoroughly unexpected treat, this museum (at the back of the Regia perfume shop) features hundreds of perfume receptacles and bottles, dating from predynastic Egypt to modern times, which you can look at but unfortunately not sniff.
☎ 93 216 01 46
🖥 www.museodel perfume.com ✉ Passeig de Gràcia 39, L'Eixample
€ free ⏰ 10.30am-1.30pm & 4.30-8pm Mon-Fri, 10.30am-1.30pm Sat Ⓜ Passeig de Gràcia ♿ fair

Museu d'Història de Catalunya (5, G6)
Inside the modernised warehouses of the Palau de Mar building, this museum is a hectic (and somewhat partisan) interactive exploration of 2000 years of Catalan history, from Roman times to the present day. Pick up a guide in English at reception and don't miss

the view from the top-floor restaurant.
☎ 93 225 47 00
🖥 www.mhcat.net
✉ Plaça de Pau Vila 3, Port Vell € €3/2.10
⏰ 10am-7pm Tue & Thu-Sat, 10am-8pm Wed, 10am-2.30pm Sun & hols
Ⓜ Barceloneta
♿ excellent

Museu Egipci (6, C4)
This surprising private collection features more than 500 exhibits, including ceramics, mummies, friezes, jewellery, masks and statuettes from ancient Egypt.
☎ 93 488 01 88
🖥 www.fundclos.com
✉ Carrer de València 284, L'Eixample € €5.50/4.50
⏰ 10am-8pm Mon-Sat, 10am-2pm Sun Ⓜ Passeig de Gràcia ♿ good

Museu Etnològic (1, B1)
Only tiny chunks of this vast collection of ethnological exhibits from non-European cultures are shown at any time. The museum presents them in context rather than just as exotic objects. In 2004, what may become a permanent display, Ètnic, opened. It presents a series of themes on traditional societies from around the

world, ranging from taboos to religions.
☎ 93 424 68 07 ✉ Passeig de Santa Madrona, Montjuïc € €3/free, free 1st Sun of month
⏰ 10am-2pm Wed & Fri-Sun, 10am-2pm & 3-7pm Tue & Thu 🚌 55 ♿ fair

Museu Frederic Marès (3, C2) Within these centuries-old walls resides a mind-boggling collection of everyday items, art and medieval Spanish sculpture amassed by Frederic Marès i Deulovol (1893–1991), sculptor, traveller and hoarder extraordinaire. Considering its scope, the collection is presented remarkably cohesively, although you may still need to catch your breath in the delightful courtyard café.
☎ 93 310 58 00 🖥 www .museumares.bcn.es
✉ Plaça de Sant Iu 5-6, Barri Gòtic € €3, free afternoons Wed & 1st Sun of month ⏰ 10am-7pm Tue-Sat, 10am-3pm Sun & hols Ⓜ Jaume I ♿ fair

Museu Militar (1, C2)
An assortment of weapons, uniforms, armour, tin soldiers and instruments of war from around the world make up this sombre collection,

housed in an 18th-century fortress overlooking Barcelona (and used more often for bombarding the city than defending it). The view is magnificent.
☎ 93 329 86 13 ✉ Castell de Montjuïc € €2.50 🕑 9.30am-5pm Tue-Sun Nov–mid-Mar, 9.30am-8pm Tue-Sun mid-Mar–Oct 🚌 PM ♿ fair

Museu Tèxtil i d'Indumentària (8, B1) Fashion victims with a sense of history will appreciate this millennia-long march-past of clobber. Inside the 13th-century mansion you are first confronted by 4th-century Coptic Egyptian textiles. The most engaging part of the collection takes you through the salons of Europe from the 17th century to the 1930s.
☎ 93 319 76 03 💻 www.museutextil .bcn.es ✉ Carrer de Montcada 12-14, La Ribera € €3.50, free 1st Sun of month 🕑 10am-6pm Tue-Sat, 10am-3pm Sun & hols Ⓜ Jaume I ♿ fair

CHURCHES & CATHEDRALS

Capella d'En Marcús (5, G3) This often unnoticed and neglected Romanesque chapel was built in the 12th century to provide shelter and alms to travellers who arrived after the city gates had closed for the night. It is only open for worship and has no regular schedule.
✉ Placeta d'En Marcús, La Ribera Ⓜ Jaume I

Església de Betlem (5, C2) Constructed in baroque style for the Jesuits in the late-17th and early-18th centuries, the 'Church of Jerusalem' was once considered the most splendid of Barcelona's few baroque offerings. Its exterior still makes a powerful impression, but arsonists destroyed much of its interior in 1936.
☎ 93 318 38 23 ✉ La Rambla dels Estudis € free 🕑 9am-2pm & 6-9pm Ⓜ Liceu

Església de Sant Pau del Camp (5, A5) Barcelona's oldest church, 'St Paul in the Fields' provides a peaceful haven in the occasionally repellent El Raval district. The church was founded by monks in the 9th century, when its location was a world away from the city. Though the squat little rural-looking building shows its age, it has some wonderful Visigothic decoration on its doorway and a fine Romanesque cloister.
☎ 93 441 00 01 ✉ Carrer de Sant Pau 101, El Raval 🕑 cloister 5-8pm Mon & Wed-Sat except public hols Ⓜ Paral.lel

Visit the 9th century at the Església de Sant Pau del Camp

Churches Burning

The conscription of young Catalans for Spain's imperialist war in Morocco lit the fuse of anarchism among disaffected workers in Barcelona in 1909. Protests and strikes spilled over into full-scale rioting against the establishment, and 70 churches, including the Església de Santa Maria del Mar (p12), were torched during what came to be known as Setmana Tràgica (Tragic Week). The anarchists attracted much popular support and when the Civil War broke out in 1936 they again vented their spleen on the churches, raiding and gutting everything from La Sagrada Família (p8) to the Església de Santa Maria del Pi (below).

Església de Sant Pere de les Puelles (5, G1)

Although altered beyond recognition since the Visigoths founded it, this fortress-like church has a remarkable history. When the Moors invaded in the 10th century the *puelles* (an order of young nuns renowned for their beauty) are said to have cut off their own noses to protect themselves from attack. Unfazed, the invaders added insult to injury by chopping off their heads as well.

☎ 93 268 07 42
✉ Plaça de Sant Pere, La Ribera ◷ 10am-1pm & 6-8.30pm Mon-Sat, 10am-2pm Sun
Ⓜ Arc de Triomf

Església de Santa Anna (5, D1)

Starting life as a simple Romanesque chapel in the 12th century, this tranquil house of worship is set off bustling Carrer de Santa Anna on a little square of its own. The deliciously silent and cool Gothic cloister encloses a leafy garden and a fountain.

☎ 93 301 35 76 ✉ Carrer de Santa Anna, Barri Gòtic ◷ 9am-1pm & 6.30-8.30pm Ⓜ Catalunya

Església de Santa Maria del Pi (5, D3)

This striking church, built between 1322 and 1453, is a classic of Catalan Gothic, with an imposing façade, a wide interior, no aisles and single nave. The beautiful rose window above its entrance is thought to be the world's largest. The name Pi comes from a lone pine tree that stood in the square in the Middle Ages – a descendant still stands there today.

☎ 93 318 47 43
✉ Plaça del Pi, Barri Gòtic ◷ 8.30am-1pm & 4.30-9pm Ⓜ Liceu

Temple del Sagrat Cor (4, C1)

Crowning Tibidabo, and seen from many parts of the city, this church was built by way of atonement for the Setmana Tràgica (see boxed text 'Churches Burning', left) of 1909 and modelled on the Sacré Coeur in Paris. It is vilified by aesthetes but has a **lift** (€1.50; ◷ 10am-2pm & 3-7pm) to the roof's staggering views.

☎ 93 307 14 17
✉ Plaça del Tibidabo ◷ 8am-7pm Ⓡ FGC Avinguda del Tibidabo, then tram Tramvia Blau, then funicular

In contemplative mood in the Barri Gòtic

PLAÇAS, PARKS & PUBLIC SPACES

Antic Hospital de la Santa Creu (5, C3) died at this 15th-century hospital, which now houses Catalonia's national library (take a look at the magnificent vaulted reading room) and an arts school. It has a delightful, if somewhat dilapidated, colonnaded courtyard, where you can hang out listening to music students practising on the steps while resisting the charms of local homeless people offering booze and wisdom. The **chapel** (☎ 93 442 71 71; ☽ noon-2pm & 4-8pm Tue-Sat, 11am-2pm Sun) of the former hospital is often the scene for temporary exhibitions.

☎ 93 270 23 00
✉ Carrer de l'Hospital 56, El Raval ☽ library 9am-8pm Mon-Fri, 9am-2pm Sat Ⓜ Liceu

Jardí Botànic (1, B2) This botanic garden concentrates on a 'Mediterranean' flora theme, with thousands of species that thrive in similar climates all over the world, from Spain to Turkey, Australia to South Africa and California to Chile.

☎ 93 426 49 35 ⌨ www .jardibotanic.bcn.es
✉ Carrer del Doctor Font i Quer, Montjuïc € €4/2 ☽ 10am-8pm Apr-Oct, 10am-5pm Nov-Mar
🚌 50, 61 & PM ⓑ fair

Jardins de Mossèn Costa i Llobera (4, G6) A longish wander downhill from the Castell de Montjuïc, these gardens are of particular

interest for the collection of tropical and desert plants – including a veritable forest of cacti.

✉ Montjuïc ☽ 10am-sunset ⓑ fair

La Rambla del Raval (5, B4) As part of the city's plan to clean up El Raval, this broad pedestrian area was created in 2000 as a breath of fresh air for the congested neighbourhood. At first serving as a welcome spot for a bit of cricket by local Pakistani youth, it is now gradually attracting interest as kebab shops and bars line up for business. Take the weight off at one of the outdoor tables.

✉ El Raval Ⓜ Liceu, Paral.lel ⓑ good

Parc de Collserola (4, A1) Some 8000 hectares of parkland spread out in the hilly country southwest of Tibidabo, forming a marvellous escape hatch for city folk needing a little nearby nature. Pick up

information at the Centre d'Informació.

☎ 93 280 35 52
✉ Carretera de l'Església 92 ☽ Centre d'Informació 9.30am-3pm 🚈 FGC Baixador de Vallvidrera

Parc d'Espanya Industrial (4, D5) Maligned by many, this playfully postmodern park comprises what look like galactic watchtowers overlooking a boating lake and a dragon sculpture that's popular with kiddies. It's transformed when illuminated at night and worth a look if you're waiting for a train at Estació Sants.

✉ Carrer de Sant Antoni, Sants ☽ 10am-sunset Ⓜ Sants Estació ⓑ fair

Passeig Marítim de la Barceloneta (4, J5) This 1.25km promenade along the beach from La Barceloneta to Port Olímpic, through an area that used to look like a railway junkyard, is now a popular spot for in-line skaters, although

---

A Fine Eixample

Ildefons Cerdà is the man responsible for the revolutionary design of the grid-like Eixample (Extension) into which Barcelona grew in the 19th century. However, developers disregarded the more utopian features of his design, which called for building on only two sides of each block and the provision of gardens within. Now, nearly 150 years later, the city is trying to reclaim a handful of these public spaces. The garden (and toddlers' pool in summer) around the Torre de les Aïgues water tower (4, G3) at Carrer de Roger de Llúria 56 offers a peek at how perfect Cerdà's plan could have been.

people without wheeled aid also stroll about. The growing contingent of bars and restaurants along the beach make it more tempting still.

✉ La Barceloneta Ⓜ Ciutadella Vila Olímpica ♿ good

Plaça de Catalunya (5, D1)
Surrounded by banks and department stores, this huge square connects the cities old and new and is the hub of Barcelona's human and pigeon life. Post-siesta it's often standing room only among the sculptures and fountains. The most imposing of the former, by Josep Subirachs, pays homage to Francesc Macià, one-time president of the Generalitat prior to the Civil War. On summer evenings Peruvian buskers often do their rhythm thing.

✉ L'Eixample Ⓜ Catalunya ♿ fair

Plaça de George Orwell (5, D4) Dubbed 'Plaça del Trippy' (in a reference to controlled substances) by the effervescent crowd that

Plaça de Sant Josep Oriol's a feelgood kind of place (opposite)

socialises here, this triangular space seems to be in a custody battle between tourists, students, new-age hippies, dealers and the homeless contingent. What would George have made of it?

✉ Barri Gòtic Ⓜ Liceu ♿ fair

Plaça de la Vila de Madrid (5, D2) Recently renovated after years of neglect, the square that takes the name of Barcelona's arch rival is the site of a series of excavated Roman tombs – this ancient

cemetery was beside the main road out of town in the days of Barcino.

✉ Barri Gòtic Ⓜ Catalunya ♿ fair

Plaça de Rius i Taulet (7, B3) This atmospheric square is dominated by a clock tower adorned with signs of the zodiac. The soul of Gràcia and the site of its 19th-century town hall, it is also a popular meeting place for locals embarked on a long night of mischief.

✉ Gràcia Ⓜ Diagonal, Fontana ♿ fair

Hanging out in Gràcia

You'd never know that Gràcia, long a separate working-class town, was only absorbed by Barcelona in the 19th century. With its crisscross patchwork of narrow and sometimes noisy lanes, Gràcia has maintained a flavour all its own. There's little in the way of sights, but the place, which went slightly bohemian in the 1970s and has retained some of that cachet, bubbles with life. Check out the Modernista market at **Plaça de la Llibertat** (7, A2) and the more down-to-earth produce market to the east, the **Mercat de l'Abaceria Central** (7, C3). Take a look at **Casa Vicenç** (4, E2; Carrer de les Carolines 22; no admittance; FGC Plaça Molina), a curious house designed by Gaudí and still in private hands. The best is the bustling life in the bars and eateries, many of which are gathered around a network of squares – the busiest are **Plaça del Sol** (7, B2) and **Plaça de la Virreina** (7, C1).

**Plaça de Sant Felip Neri
(3, A2)** A fountain provides
a watery ambient music for
this peaceful square with
a dark history, lying in the
shadow of the church of the
same name. The pockmarked
walls of the church are testa-
ment to its function as a Civil
War execution yard, and are
a silent monument to those
who died here.
☒ **Barri Gòtic** Ⓜ **Liceu**
♿ **fair**

**Plaça de Sant Jaume
(3, B3)** *El lugar donde se
cocina todo* (the place where
everything gets cooked),
this square has been the
centre of Barcelona's civic
life since the Romans first
hung their helmets here.
☒ **Barri Gòtic** Ⓜ **Jaume I**
♿ **fair**

**Plaça de Sant Josep Oriol
& Plaça del Pi (5, D3)**
These atmospheric con-
joined squares nestle be-
neath the towering Església
de Santa Maria del Pi. They
are both lined with cafés,
buskers and cheerful souls,
and reached by numerous
quaint narrow streets.
☒ **Barri Gòtic** Ⓜ **Liceu**
♿ **fair**

Plaça de Sant Just (5, E4)
A captivating medieval
square with a peculiarly posi-
tive vibe and a water fountain dating from 1367, this
is also the site where Gaudí,
on his way to a service in the
Església de Sant Just i Pastor,
insisted on speaking Catalan
to a policeman and ended
up spending a day in the
slammer for his trouble.
☒ **Barri Gòtic** Ⓜ **Jaume I**
♿ **fair**

**Plaça de Santa Maria
del Mar (8, A3)** This is
one of the city's pretti-
est spaces and offers the
perfect vantage point from
which to view the stun-
ning church of the same
name while enjoying some
delightful terrace dining
and sipping.
☒ **La Ribera** Ⓜ **Jaume I**
♿ **fair**

Plaça del Rei (3, C2)
In this wholly preserved
medieval courtyard,
King Fernando reputedly
greeted Christopher
Columbus upon his return
from discovering the New
World. It is surrounded
by buildings of the Palau
Reial, most of which are
now open to visitors as
the Museu d'Història de la
Ciutat (p13).
☒ **Barri Gòtic** Ⓜ **Jaume I**
♿ **fair**

Plaça del Sol (7, B2)
This gregarious square –
where the young folk of
Gràcia converge in the
evenings – is lined with
bars and eateries, and is

a great place to be when
alfresco is paramount.
☒ **Gràcia** Ⓜ **Fontana**
♿ **fair**

Plaça dels Àngels (5, B2)
Conceived as a parade
ground for an artsy crowd,
this wide space in front of
the Macba (p28) has been
overrun by gleeful skaters
and trick-bikers who seem
to have more spills than
thrills on the low wall.
☒ **El Raval**
Ⓜ **Universitat** ♿ **fair**

Plaça Reial (5, D4)
A pretty, expansive square
with neoclassical façades,
palm trees, and numerous
restaurants and bars. Once
notorious for poverty and
crime, it still has a jaunty
edginess. Cops stand
on nonchalant patrol as
vagrants vie with tipsy
tourists for the amused
attention of the casual
observer. The elegant
lampposts were Gaudí's
first commission in the big
smoke.
☒ **Barri Gòtic** Ⓜ **Liceu**
♿ **fair**

I suddenly feel so small…Plaça del Rei

PUBLIC ART

Barcelona's wealth of public artworks is the result of an innovative project started by the city council in the late 1970s to revitalise individual neighbourhoods. With the offer of a blank canvas and all expenses paid, artists from around the world worked for a fraction of their market rates and created these engaging pieces of art to decorate the city.

Barcelona Head (5, F5)

Designed by the American pop artist Roy Lichtenstein in 1992, this 14m sculpture just back from the marinas of Port Vell is impossible to miss. The broken ceramic coating is believed to be a homage to Gaudí, but the overall impression, as was always the case with Lichtenstein's work, is of a Sunday newspaper comic-strip character.

✉ **Passeig de Colom, Port Vell** Ⓜ **Barceloneta**

David i Goliat (4, J4)

Beneath the two skyscrapers of the Olympic village, Antoni Llena's wonderful sculpture from 1993 honours the poor who were uprooted from this neighbourhood. It consists of a large metal sheet shaped like a mask and suspended 20m up on three steel tubes.

✉ **Plaça dels Voluntaris Olímpics, Port Olímpic** Ⓜ **Ciutadella Vila Olímpica**

Dona i Ocell (4, D5)

One of the symbols of Barcelona, 'Woman and Bird' was Joan Miró's last large sculpture, inaugurated in 1981, the year of his death, in what is now known as Parc Joan Miró. It was made in collaboration with the ceramist Joan Gardy Artigas. Locals still refer to the rather drab space as Parc de l'Escorxador (Abbatoir Park) because it used to be a slaughterhouse for the nearby one-time bullring.

✉ **Parc Joan Miró, Sants** Ⓜ **Tarragona**

El Desconsol (5, J4)

One of the few examples of public Modernista statuary in town, Despair (1906) is curiously located outside the regional Catalan parliament. Perhaps the choice of site was a wry comment by sculptor Josep Llimona on the state of local politics. Some would say the comment is equally pertinent today.

✉ **Parc de la Ciutadella, La Ribera** Ⓜ **Barceloneta**

Gat (5, B4)

Popular with the locals, this giant and tubby tabby is the work of Colombian artist Fernando Botero and was unveiled in 1992. It was shunted around a bit before arriving at its present spot. The statue's biggest

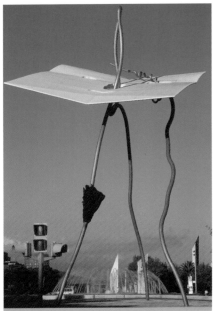

A homage to the dispossessed – David i Goliat

headache are the vandals who occasionally amuse themselves by breaking off his whiskers!

✉ **La Rambla del Raval, El Raval** Ⓜ **Drassanes**

Homenatge a l'Exposició Universal del 1888 (5, H3)

Loathed as an eyesore by many Barcelonins – and included here just out of devilment – this homage to urban transformation (1991) by Antoni Clavè can be found in Barcelona's oldest park, the site of the 1888 Universal Exhibition.

✉ **Parc de la Ciutadella, La Ribera** Ⓜ **Arc de Triomf**

La Dama del Paraigua

(5, J5) The rather curious late-19th-century statue of a society dame parading with an umbrella was done in 1885 by Joan Roig and was quite a hit at the time. Roig was a busy man. In addition to his sculpture he was contracted to produce much of the statuary on the façade of the Catedral (p15), which for all its medieval air was completed in the 19th century.

✉ **Parc de la Ciutadella, La Ribera** Ⓜ **Barceloneta**

Mosaic de Miró – beautiful and resiliant

L'Estel Ferit (4, H5)

American Rebecca Horn's striking tribute to La Barceloneta (aka *Homenatge a la Barceloneta*) stands on the beach. The eye-catching column of rusted iron and glass cubes is illuminated at night.

✉ **Platja de Sant Sebastià, La Barceloneta** Ⓜ **Barceloneta**

Mosaic de Miró (5, D3)

Smack bang in the middle of La Rambla, this colourful mosaic painted by Joan Miró in 1976 (he also signed one of the bricks) gives you the rare chance to trample a work of art underfoot without raising anyone's hackles.

✉ **Plaça de la Boqueria, La Rambla** Ⓜ **Liceu**

Peix (4, J4) American

Frank Gehry's smooth and hollow copper Fish sculpture, which fairly scintillates in the sunlight, was installed for the Olympics and can be admired all along the beaches and promenades.

✉ **Port Olímpic** Ⓜ **Ciutadella Vila Olímpica**

A New Seaside Suburb

After the success of the 1992 Olympics, Barcelona decided to roll the dice and try again with another, ill-defined international event in 2004, the Fòrum Universal de les Cultures. A five-month-long talk-fest-cum-concert-programme, it failed to make quite the same impact as the games. Out of it grew a major urban-planning project, the waterside Diagonal Mar district east of Port Olímpic, with high-rise apartments and hotels, a marina, carefully planned parks, a convention centre and Herzog & de Meuron's strangely alluring triangular Edifici Fòrum. It's too early to tell if it will develop a soul or remain a cold, distant residential ghetto. Barcelona architecture doyen Oriol Bohigas has damned it as an urban disaster.

NOTABLE BUILDINGS & MONUMENTS

Ajuntament (3, B3) Also known as the Casa de la Ciutat, this town hall has been the seat of city power since the 14th century and has a Catalan Gothic side façade on Carrer de la Ciutat. Belying its blandly renovated neoclassical front is a spectacular interior featuring a majestic staircase and the splendidly restored Saló de Cent (Chamber of the One Hundred).
☎ 010 ⊠ Plaça de Sant Jaume, Barri Gòtic € free ⏰ 10am-2pm Sat & Sun Ⓜ Jaume I ♿ fair

Arc de Triomf (5, H1)
This curious Josep Vilaseca monument, with its Islamic-style brickwork, was the ceremonial entrance to the 1888 Universal Exhibition, Barcelona's first spirited attempt to put itself on the world map. Exactly what triumph it commemorates isn't clear – probably just getting the thing built in time for the exhibition.
⊠ Passeig de Lluís Companys, La Ribera Ⓜ Arc de Triomf

Bellesguard (4, C1)
In typical Gaudí fashion, exposed brick, wrought iron and a sense of fairytale playfulness combine to give this still private mansion, built in 1909, an unreal feel. It's a bit of a hike and private property, so you need to be a fan of obscure things off beaten tracks.
⊠ Carrer de Bellesguard, Zona Alta Ⓡ FGC Avinguda del Tibidabo

Casa Calvet (4, G3)
Gaudí's first apartment block and most conventional building is interesting because it won him the only award of his life, the city council's prize for the best building of 1900. It's sober and straight from the outside, but some hints of whimsy can be seen in the ground-floor restaurant (see p78).
☎ 93 412 40 12 ⊠ Carrer de Casp 48, L'Eixample Ⓜ Urquinaona

Casa de l'Ardiaca (3, B1)
This 16th-century house is home to the city's archives and has a supremely serene courtyard, renovated by Domènech i Montaner in 1902, when the building was owned by the lawyers' college. Montaner also designed the postal slot, which is adorned with swallows and a tortoise, said to represent the swiftness of truth and the plodding pace of justice. You can get a good glimpse at some stout Roman wall in here.
⊠ Carrer de Santa Llúcia 1, Barri Gòtic ⏰ 9am-9pm Mon-Fri, 9am-2pm Sat Ⓜ Jaume I

Casa de les Punxes (6, C2)
Puig i Cadafalch could have been eating too much cheese late at night when he created this neo-Gothic fantasy, which was built between 1903 and 1905. Officially the Casa Terrades, its pointed turrets earned it the popular nickname Casa de les Punxes (House of the Spikes).
⊠ Avinguda Diagonal 420, L'Eixample Ⓜ Diagonal

Farmàcia Nordbeck (4, G3) For whatever reason, pharmacies and Modernisme had a tight relationship in l'Eixample. With its stained glass, dark wood and sinuous design, this 1905 building is a prime example of how asking a stranger for haemorrhoid cream needn't be such a trauma.
⊠ Carrer d'Ausiàs Marc 31, L'Eixample Ⓜ Urquinaona

Gran Teatre del Liceu (5, C4) Built in 1847, burned to a crisp in 1994 and resurrected five years later, this is Barcelona's grand operatic stage. It can seat up to 2300 in its

Roman Walls
Of course, the city's first architects of note were the Romans who built a town here in the 1st century BC. Large relics of the 3rd- and 4th-century walls that marked the boundary of this town can still be seen in the Barri Gòtic, particularly at **Plaça de Ramon de Berenguer el Gran** (3, C2) and by the northern end of **Carrer del Sotstinent Navarro** (3, C3).

auditorium, where the classic 19th-century stalls have been restored and combined with hi-tech stage equipment. If you can't make a show, come for a wander around, preferably with a guide.

☎ 93 485 99 14 ⌨ www .liceubarcelona.com ✉ La Rambla dels Caputxins 51-59 € €3.50, guided tour adult/student/child under 10 €5.50/4/free ☆ guided tours 10am, unguided visits 11.30am, noon & 1pm Ⓜ Liceu ⚐ good

Arc de Triomf – success on its own terms (see opposite)

Hospital de la Santa Creu i de Sant Pau (4, G1)

A Domènech i Montaner masterpiece, begun in 1901 and finished by his son in 1930, this uniquely chirpy hospital is a gargantuan Modernista landmark comprising 48 unique and lavishly decorated pavilions. Feign illness or just wander around the gardens. The hospital wards are being transferred to more modern facilities, and the site will eventually house a museum on medicine and Montaner.

✉ Carrer de Cartagena, El Guinardó Ⓜ Hospital de Sant Pau

L'Anella Olímpica & Estadi Olímpic (1, B2)

For sports fans, L'Anella Olímpica (Olympic Ring) is the group of installations built for the main events of the 1992 Olympics. They include the Estadi Olímpic, which is open to the public when Espanyol (the 'other' football team) isn't getting whipped.

✉ Avinguda de l'Estadi, Montjuïc € free

☆ 10am-6pm Oct-Apr, 10am-8pm May-Sep Ⓜ Paral.lel, then Funicular de Montjuïc

Llotja (5, F5) This 14th-century building housed the old stock exchange and for a time an arts school attended by Picasso and Miró. The exterior is 18th-century neoclassical, but there is a superb original Gothic hall inside. Unfortunately, it is off limits to tourists.

✉ Carrer del Consolat de Mar 2, La Ribera Ⓜ Barceloneta, Jaume I

Manzana de la Discordia (6, B4)

If we didn't think we knew better, we'd be tempted to believe that some wiseacre in the Barcelona town hall back in the 1900s thought it would be amusing to have the three top Modernista architects line up for posterity. On one block of Passeig de Gràcia are located three incredibly disparate houses: Gaudí's gaudy Casa Batlló (p17), Puig i Cadafalch's

medieval–Dutch–looking Casa Amatller at No 41 and Domènech i Montaner's more rounded Casa Lleo Morera at No 35. The latter two can be admired only from the outside.

✉ Passeig de Gràcia, L'Eixample Ⓜ Passeig de Gràcia

Mercat del Born (5, G4)

After decades of silence beneath the wrought-iron roof of what had been the city's main wholesale market since the 1870s, the site suddenly gave a yelp in the early 2000s as a whole swath of late-medieval Barcelona was uncovered. This was part of the area flattened to make way for the sinister Ciutadella in the 18th century. Plans to build a library here have been scrapped. Instead, a museum and cultural centre will occupy the spot, so the excavations will be preserved.

✉ Plaça Comercial, La Ribera € free ☆ 10am-8pm Sat, 10am-3pm Sun Ⓜ Barceloneta

Ruta del Modernisme

This ticket (€3, valid for 30 days) provides a half-price discount to the **Palau de la Música Catalana** (p24), **Fundació Antoni Tàpies** (p27) and **Museu de Zoologia** (p29). More interesting is the Modernisme itinerary map and guide booklet. You can pick the ticket up in the **Casa de Amatller** (6, B4; ☎ 93 488 01 39; Passeig de Gràcia 41), one of the three Modernista buildings of the Manzana de la Discordia (p39).

Monument a Colom

(5, C6) Centuries after he stumbled across the Americas while looking for India, Columbus was honoured with this 60m monument, built for the Universal Exhibition in 1888. It looks like he's urging the tourist throngs to go elsewhere, but you can catch a lift to the soles of his feet for a fine view.

☎ 93 302 52 24
✉ Plaça del Portal de la Pau, Port Vell € lift €2/1.30 ☉ 9am-8.30pm Jun-Sep, 10am-6.30pm Oct-May Ⓜ Drassanes

Palau de la Generalitat

(3, B3) This seat of Catalan government was adapted from several Gothic mansions in the early 15th century and extended over time as it grew in importance. Its Gothic side façade on Carrer del Bisbe Irurita features a wonderful relief of St George that was made by Pere Joan in 1418. Visiting times to see its grand interior are limited.

☎ 012 ✉ Plaça de Sant Jaume, Barri Gòtic € free ☉ free guided tours 10.30am 2nd & 4th Sun of month (bring ID) Ⓜ Jaume I & good

Palau del Baró Quadras

(6, B2) Remodelled by Puig i Cadafalch between 1902 and 1904, the palace currently houses the Casa Asia cultural centre. It has fine stained glass and its façade is ornamented with detailed neo-Gothic carvings.

☎ 93 238 73 37
🖳 www.casaasia.es
✉ Avinguda Diagonal 373 € free ☉ 10am-8pm Tue-Sat, 10am-2pm Sun Ⓜ Diagonal

Pavelló Mies van der Rohe

(1, A1) This is a replica of a structure erected for – and demolished with – the 1929 World Exhibition. In hindsight it was considered to be a milestone of modern architecture and was rebuilt in 1986. It is Mies van der Rohe's vision of a new urban environment, with a light and airy design comprising horizontal planes.

☎ 93 423 40 16
🖳 www.miesbcn.com
✉ Avinguda del Marquès de Comillas, Montjuïc

€ adult/student/child under 18 €3/1.50/free ☉ 10am-8pm Ⓜ Espanya & good

Poble Espanyol

(1, A1) Something of an impostor in this section, the 'Spanish Village' was put together for the 1929 World Exhibition. It comprises replicas of famous buildings and examples of traditional architecture from all over Spain. For a tourist trap, it's quite engaging, but its craft shops, restaurants and bars share the unfortunate distinction of being overpriced.

☎ 93 508 63 30
🖳 www.poble-espanyol.com ✉ Avinguda del Marquès de Comillas € adult/concession/child under 12 €7/5/3.90 ☉ 9am-8pm Mon, 9am-2am Tue-Thu, 9am-4am Fri & Sat, 9am-midnight Sun Ⓜ Espanya & good

Torre de Collserola

(4, A1) This 288m telecommunications tower, designed by Britain's Sir Norman Foster, was built to bring the events of the 1992 Olympics to television viewers around the world. A glass lift shoots up to an observation deck at 115m that affords splendid views of Tibidabo and the city.

☎ 93 406 93 54
🖳 www.torrede collserola.com ✉ Carretera de Vallvidrera € €4.60/3.30 ☉ 11am-2.30pm & 3.30-7pm Wed-Sun 🚆 FGC Avinguda del Tibidabo, then tram Tramvia Blau, then funicular & fair

QUIRKY BARCELONA

Espai Urbà (5, E4) Head straight for the two seats with screens that look suspiciously like arcade games. No, it isn't Doom, but rather an interactive programme that allows you to make simulated flights over Barcelona. If you can drag yourself away from these gadgets, wander around this otherwise celebratory didactic display and get a feel for the city's big urban projects in the coming years.
☎ 93 402 73 12
✉ Carrer de la Ciutat 2
€ free ⏰ 10am-8pm Tue-Fri, 10am-2pm Sat & Sun Ⓜ Jaume I ♿ fair

Museu de Carrosses Fúnebres (4, H3) A fascinating collection of horse-drawn funeral carriages (and a few motorised ones) that were used in the city from the 18th century until the 1950s. The varying degrees of ornamentation on each indicate the status of the passengers and provide a unique window into the past.
☎ 93 484 17 20
🖥 www.funeraria barcelona.com
✉ Carrer de Sancho d'Àvila 2 € free

Museu de l'Eròtica: not top of the list for school excursions

⏰ 10am-1pm & 4-6pm Mon-Fri, 10am-1pm Sat, Sun & hols Ⓜ Marina

Museu de l'Eròtica (5, D3) Falling somewhere between titillation, tawdriness and art, this private collection is devoted to sex and sexuality through the ages. The décor is pseudo-seedy, and the diverse exhibits range from exquisite Kamasutra illustrations, tribal carvings and Mapplethorpe photos to early porn movies, S&M apparatus and a 6ft wooden penis.
☎ 93 318 98 65
🖥 www.erotica -museum.com ✉ La Rambla de Sant Josep 96
€ €7.50 ⏰ 10am-midnight Jun-Sep, 11am-9pm Oct-May Ⓜ Liceu

Museu del Calçat (3, A2) Hotfoot it to this unexpected treat, the little museum of shoes: dainty ones, famous ones, weird

Touched by the Mushroom

Mr Calvet, the man who commissioned Gaudí to build Casa Calvet, was a connoisseur of mushrooms and is believed to have stimulated Gaudí's interest in all things fungi. Later in the architect's flamboyant career, particularly after Parc Güell, rumour raced around town that he was, in fact, 'touched by the mushroom'. Hallucinogenics aside, after Casa Calvet he rarely drew another straight line.

ones, Roman ones, silk ones, seamless ones, baby ones and one gigantic one made for the Monument a Colom (p40).
☎ 93 301 45 33
✉ Plaça de Sant Felip Neri 5 € €2 ⏱ 11am-2pm Tue-Sun Ⓜ Liceu

Temple Romà d'Augusti (3, B3) It's unremarkable from the outside, but this courtyard houses four Corinthian columns of Barcelona's main Roman temple, built in the 1st century in the name of Caesar Augustus.
✉ **Carrer del Paradis 10, Barri Gòtic** € free ⏱ (unreliable) 10am-2pm Mon-Sat Ⓜ Jaume I

Torre Agbar (4, H2) French architect Jean Nouvel is in the process of gracing Barcelona with its very own cucumber-shaped building, the Torre Agbar. Unlike Sir Norman Foster's Swiss Re building in London's already tower-jammed City, this shimmering and still-unfinished contribution sticks out in Barcelona's cityscape like a sore thumb.
✉ **Avinguda Diagonal 225** Ⓜ **Glòries**

BARCELONA FOR CHILDREN

Barcelona is a fairytale city crammed with all sorts of weird and wonderful stuff the likes of which most kids won't have seen before. From the street artists of La Rambla to the madcap designs of Modernista buildings, the city is awash with ageless pleasures. In addition to the specifically child-friendly sights listed on these pages, you could try the Museu Marítim (p22), the Museu del Futbol Club Barcelona (p21), Torre de Collserola (p40), L'Aquàrium (p14), the Museu d'Història de Catalunya (p30) or a visit to any of the beaches and parks. Ask at your hotel for the nearest playground and at the tourist office for details of theatre, concerts and other programmes designed for children (especially in summer).

Ferris-wheeling fun at the Parc d'Atraccions

CosmoCaixa (4, C1)
Located in a transformed Modernista building and reopened for business in late 2004, this science museum is four times bigger than the original. It's a giant, interactive paradise with knobs on (and buttons, levers and lots more besides). At the time of research, admission was free until January 2005.
☎ 93 212 60 50
✉ **Carrer de Teodor Roviralta 47-51, Zona Alta** € free ⏱ 10am-8pm, Tue-Sun Ⓡ FGC Avinguda del Tibidabo, then tram Tramvia Blau
♿ excellent

Golondrina Excursion Boats (4, G5) Kids will love the 1½ -hour jaunt around the harbour and along the beaches to the northeast tip of town aboard a *golondrina* (swallow). Shorter trips are also available (and tend to leave more often).
☎ 93 442 31 06
🖥 www.lasgolondrinas .com ✉ Moll de les Drassanes € adult/ child 11-18/child 4-10 €8.80/6.30/3.85
🕑 several outings daily
Ⓜ Drassanes

La Font Màgica (1, A1)
Delightfully over the top, the biggest of Montjuïc's famous fountains splashes into life with an irresistible summer-evening extravaganza of music and light. Whether it's to the tune of Tchaikovsky or Abba, the waterworks will make you giddy with glee.
✉ Avinguda de la Reina Maria Cristina € free
🕑 every half-hour 7-8.30pm Fri & Sat Oct-late Jun, 9.30-11.30pm Thu-Sun late Jun-Sep
Ⓜ Espanya ♿ fair

Museu de Cera (5, D5)
With a collection of 300 wax figures of famous Catalans and familiar faces from around the world, this is just as creepy as any other wax museum – something kids seem to lap up and adults frequently loathe! More horrible than any display of twisted medieval torture are the figures of Prince Charlie with Camilla.
☎ 93 317 26 49 🖥 www .museocerabcn.com
✉ Passatge de la Banca 7 € €6.65/3.75 🕑 10am-

Barcelo-little-uns

If you don't see many child facilities around it's because kids are usually treated like little adults in Barcelona. While parents don't drag them out for nights on the razzle, it's common to see toddlers out with mums and dads in restaurants until 11pm or so. Your kids will be made to feel welcome wherever you go.

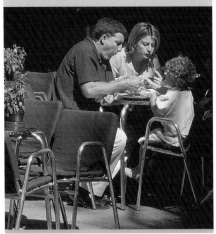

It's never too early to start dining out in Barcelona

1.30pm & 4-7.30pm Mon-Fri, 11am- 2pm & 4.30-8.30pm Sat, Sun & hols Ⓜ Drassanes

Museu de la Xocolata (5, G3) Explore the history and potential of chocolate through audiovisual displays (in English on request), touch-screen presentations, historical exhibits and the most extraordinary chocolate models of anything from grand monuments to cartoon characters – now how could anyone have the heart to take a first bite out of these? There are also cooking demonstrations, tastings and (with advance

notice) workshops where the kids can make their own models.
☎ 93 268 78 78
🖥 www.museuxocolata .com, in Catalan ✉ Plaça de Pons i Clerch s/n
€ €3.80, free 1st Mon of month 🕑 10am-7pm Mon & Wed-Sat, 10am-3pm Sun & hols
Ⓜ Jaume I

Parc d'Atraccions (4, C1)
For the Ferris-wheel ride of your life – with the bonus of panoramic views from the top of Tibidabo – make a beeline for this cherished old-fashioned funfair. It has all the usual thrills as well as the remarkable

Baby-Sitting & Childcare

Most of the medium- and upper-range hotels in Barcelona can organise a baby-sitting service for their guests' children. A company many hotels use (and which you can contact directly) is **5 Serveis** (5, C1; ☎ 93 412 56 76, mob ☎ 639-361111; Carrer de Pelai 50), which employs multilingual *canguros* (baby-sitters). Rates vary, but evenings are generally €8.70 an hour plus the cost of the baby-sitter's taxi home.

Museu d'Autòmats del Tibidabo, where you can see carnival games and gizmos dating back to the 19th century.
☎ 93 211 79 42
✉ Plaça de Tibidabo
€ 6 rides €11, access to all rides €22, children under 1.1m €9 ☼ noon-10pm or 11pm Aug, noon-5pm or 9pm Sat, Sun & hols Sep-Jul & some other days in warmer months
🚃 FGC Avinguda del Tibidabo, then tram Tramvia Blau, then funicular

Telefèric (4, G6-H5) This cable car (aka *funicular aeri*), strung out precariously across the harbour

to Montjuïc, provides a bird's-eye view of the city. The cabins float between Miramar (Montjuïc) and the Torre de Sant Sebastià (La Barceloneta).
✉ Passeig Escullera, La Barceloneta € one way/return €7.50/9
☼ 10.30am-8pm mid-Jun–mid-Sep, 10.30am-7pm Mar–mid-Jun & mid-Sep–mid-Oct, noon-5.30pm mid-Oct–Feb
Ⓜ Barceloneta 🚌 17, 39 & 64

Zoo de Barcelona (5, J4)
As thrilling or depressing as any other, this small zoo occupies the southern end of the Parc de la Ciutadella

and was for some time home to the only albino gorilla in the world. She passed on in 2003, leaving behind around 7000 critters encompassing everything from geckos to gorillas (including a pair of twins born in 2004). There are plans to move the zoo to a new spot in the El Fòrum site on the north-east coast of the city, but implementing them could take quite a while.
☎ 93 225 67 80
✉ Parc de la Ciutadella, La Ribera € €12.90/8.30
☼ 10am-7.30pm Apr-Sep, 10am-5pm Oct-Mar
Ⓜ Barceloneta
♿ fair

Great view and an easy commute – the Telefèric's prime real estate

Out & About

WALKING TOURS
Burrowing into the Barri Gòtic

Facing the **Catedral** (**1**; p15), follow the right flank of the **Palau de la Generalitat** (**2**; p40) along Carrer del Bisbe Irurita until you reach the city's administrative heart, **Plaça de Sant Jaume** (**3**; p35). Turn right along Carrer del Call, the main street of the ancient Jewish quarter or '**Call**' (**4**; p65). At No 1 Carrer de Marlet, a graffiti-daubed inscription records the death of a rabbi in AD 692, while at No 5 are the remnants of the city's **Sinagoga Major** (**5**; ☎ 93 317 07 90; www.calldebarcelona. org). Follow this street and head left up Carrer de Sant Domènec del Call. A quick right and left, and you have before you the **Església de Sant Felip Neri** (**6**; p35) dominating the quiet square of the same name. Through the arch on Carrer de Montjuïc del Bisbe turn left to retrace a few steps on

Carrer del Bisbe Irurita and cross the face of the Catedral. At Plaça de Sant Iu glide down the few steps into the **Museu Frederic Marès** (**7**; p30) and its tranquil courtyard café. Resume along Carrer dels Comtes de Barcelona, taking the next left on Baixada de Santa Clara, where you will be drawn into **Plaça del Rei** (**8**; p35). At the **Museu d'Història de la Ciutat** (**9**; p13) you can undertake an underground Roman-era walk (see Ruta del Gòtic, p51 – an eerie voyage back in time.

distance 1km duration 45mins
▶ start Ⓜ Jaume I, Avda de la Catedral
● end Ⓜ Jaume I, Plaça del Rei

Feel the power in the Plaça de Sant Jaume

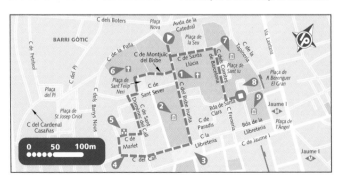

La Ribera Lowdown

Cross Via Laietana to Carrer de la Boria, part of the commercial centre of medieval Barcelona. You pass Carrer dels Mercaders (Traders' St) on your left before entering the atmospheric Plaça de la Llana, where wool was sold. The street becomes Carrer dels Corders (Ropemakers' St) and leads to the neglected **Capella d'En Marcús** (**1**; p31). Heading south from the chapel you enter the medieval Park Ave of Barcelona. Carrer de Montcada, purposely laid out as a residential avenue for the rich and richer of Barcelona's busy commercial world, is lined with their medieval and baroque mansions. Five now house the **Museu**

Step up to Santa Maria del Mar

Picasso (**2**; p10), the **Museu Tèxtil i d'Indumentària** (**3**; p31) and the **Museu Barbier-Mueller d'Art Pre-Colombí** (**4**; p28). Stop by the Museu Picasso's refreshing courtyard café or **El Xampanyet** (**5**; p76) for *cava* (Spanish sparkling wine) and snacks. **Passeig del Born** (**6**) was a stage for jousts and executions, and is now the scene of late-night revelry – explore the bar-and-restaurant-infested side streets. At its east end is the former **Mercat del Born** (**7**; p39), one-time produce market and now archaeological site, and its west end is closed off by the magnificent Gothic outline of the **Església de Santa Maria del Mar** (**8**; p12). Head for Plaça de l'Àngel along Carrer de l'Argenteria (Silversmiths' St) to reach the metro.

distance 1.4km **duration** 1½hrs
▶ **start** Ⓜ Jaume I
● **end** Ⓜ Jaume I

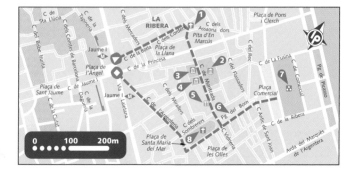

Modernista Meander

Head up Passeig de Gràcia past the **Manzana de la Discordia** (**1**; p39) on your left, **La Pedrera** (**2**; p16) a few blocks up on your right and Modernista lampposts on the way. On the corner of Avda Diagonal is an early work by Josep Puig i Cadafalch, **Palau del Baró Quadras** (**3**; p40). Opposite and to the right is Salvador Valeri's **Casa Comalat** (**4**; no admittance), which has a more playful façade at the back. Further along is Puig i Cadafalch's **Casa de les Punxes** (**5**; p38) or House of Spikes. Drop down Carrer de Roger de Llúria, detouring left along Carrer de Mallorca to Casa Thomas, now home to the design showrooms of **Bd Ediciones de Diseño** (**6**; p56). Retake Carrer de Roger de Llúria and admire the goodies in the Modernista window display of the family shop **J Murrià** (**7**; p58) at No 85. A few blocks further on, turn left into Carrer d'Ausiàs Marc. On the next corner is **Farmàcia Nordbeck** (**8**; p38), a fine Modernista pharmacy. Two extraordinary buildings on the next block are **Casa Antoni Roger** (**9**; built by Enric Sagnier in 1890; no admittance) and, further along, **Casa Antonia Burés** (**10**; built by Juli Batllevell in 1906; no admittance). Backpedal, drop down Carrer de Girona and head right into Carrer de Sant Pere més Alt until you encounter a jewel of Modernisme, the **Palau de la Música Catalana** (**11**; p24), before retiring to **Els Quatre Gats** (**12**; p70) for a bite.

distance 5.5km **duration** 3hrs
▶ **start** Ⓜ Catalunya
● **end** Ⓜ Urquinaona

Punchy: the Casa de les Punxes

The Depths of El Raval

El Raval has just enough edge for you to want to keep your wallet well clasped in your front pocket. Starting at the seafaring **Museu Marítim** (**1**; p22), follow Avda de les Drassanes and turn right along narrow and often urine-perfumed Carrer de l'Arc del Teatre. Spill left onto La Rambla (at night you'll be observed by groups of pouting prostitutes) and left again into Carrer Nou de la Rambla. Wander past one of Gaudí's early commissions, **Palau Güell** (**2**; p26) and a more rollicking Modernista landmark, the evergreen **London Bar** (**3**; p86). The busiest gathering of ladies of the night hangs along Carrer de Sant Ramon to the right, but you'll push on to Avda del Paral.lel. This was once a bit of a theatreland but has lost its twinkle. Turn right at Carrer de l'Abat Safont and right again into Carrer de Sant Pau for a rare Romanesque relic, the **Església de Sant Pau del Camp** (**4**; p31). After passing the broad **Rambla del Raval** (**5**), host to several decent watering holes with outside tables, and a classic 19th-century tavern, **Bar Marsella** (**6**; p84), slip past the drug abusers, pimps and dealers and shimmy up Carrer d'En Robador (Robber St, until recently lined by cheap-and-nasty girlie bars) to the 15th-century **Antic Hospital de la Santa Creu** (**7**; p33), now the Catalan national library. Cross its grounds and push north along Carrer dels Àngels to the sparkling **Museu d'Art Contemporani de Barcelona** (**8**; p28).

distance 3km **duration** 2hrs	
▶ **start** Ⓜ Drassanes	
● **end** Ⓜ Universitat	

A mid-walk beacon: London Bar

DAY TRIPS
Figueres (2, C1)

You've checked out Picasso and Miró in Barcelona, so how can you miss the chance to visit the doyen of daftness, Salvador Dalí? The spiritual centre of Europe (as Dalí liked to refer to it) is his extraordinary project the **Teatre-Museu Dalí** (☎ 972 67 75 00; www.salvador-dali.org; incl Dalí Joies €9/6.50, night sessions €8; 🕘 9am-7.45pm Jul-Sep, 10.30am-5.45pm Tue-Sun rest of year, night sessions 10pm-12.30am most of summer), created in the otherwise rather dull town of his birth, Figueres. The museum comprises three floors of tricks, illusions and absurdity where even the catalogue is designed to confuse. The final exhibit, and the plainest one by far, is Dalí's tomb, where the artist has been encased since 1989. Part of the collection is **Dalí Joies**, showcasing exquisite jewellery designed by the master. Visits to a couple of other museums will round out the day's excursion.

INFORMATION

129km northeast of Barcelona

🚉 Figueres; 1¾-2hrs

ℹ tourist office (☎ 972 50 31 55; Plaça del Sol)

✗ La Churraskita (☎ 972 50 15 52; Carrer Magre 5)

Form from function at Teatre-Museu Dalí

Girona (2, C2)

Huddled in multicoloured confusion on the banks of the Onyar, this medieval town makes a delightful stop on the way to or from Figueres. The majestic **Catedral** (☎ 972 21 44 26; Plaça de la Catedral; €3; 🕘 10am-2pm & 4-7pm Tue-Sat Mar-Jun, 10am-8pm Tue-Sat Jul-Sep, 10am-2pm & 4-6pm Tue-Sat Oct-Feb, 10am-2pm Sun & hols year-round), with its irregular Romanesque cloister and powerful Gothic interior, lords it over the rest of the town. Study Girona's history at the **Museu d'Història de la Ciutat** (☎ 972 22 22 29; Carrer de la Força 27; €2; 🕘 10am-2pm & 5-7pm Tue-Sat, 10am-2pm Sun) and wander the narrow streets of the medieval Jewish district around Carrer de la Força. Cross the river for the engaging **Museu del Cinema** (☎ 972 41 27 77; Carrer del Perill 5; €3; 🕘 10am-8pm Tue-Sun May-Sep, 10am-6pm Tue-Fri, 10am-8pm Sat, 11am-3pm Sun Oct-Apr).

INFORMATION

91km northeast of Barcelona

🚉 Girona; 1¼-1½hrs

ℹ tourist office (☎ 972 22 65 75; La Rambla de la Llibertat 1)

✗ Restaurant Albereda (☎ 972 22 60 02; Carrer de l'Albereda 9)

Sitges (2, A3)

Only half an hour from Barcelona, Sitges is a unique resort that in summer attracts hordes of fashionable city folk and a huge international gay set. It was a trendy hangout for artists and bohemians in the 1890s and has remained one of Spain's most unconventional resorts ever since. It's no

INFORMATION
41km southwest of Barcelona
🚃 Sitges; 30mins
ℹ️ tourist office (☎ 93 894 42 51; Carrer de Sínia Morera 1)
✕ Al Fresco (☎ 93 894 06 00; Carrer de Pau Barrabeig 4)

less attractive in winter, although you won't have much company as you cavort between its three **museums** (☎ 93 894 03 64; admission to all museums €5.40/3; ☯ 10am-1.30pm & 3-6.30pm Tue-Fri, 10am-7pm Sat, 10am-3pm Sun Oct-Jun, 10am-2pm & 5-9pm Tue-Sun Jul-Sep), admire the sun-bleached baroque church that stands on a promontory over the beach, soak up the village atmosphere and wonder if it's too cold for a dip at the nude beach southwest of town.

Montserrat (2, A2)

Montserrat (Serrated Mountain) is the spiritual heart of Catalonia and your best opportunity to enjoy awesome scenery on a day trip from Barcelona. Comprising a massif of limestone pinnacles rising precipitously over gorges, this wondrous place has drawn hermits (er, independent travellers) since the 5th century. Perched up here is a monastery and 12th-century chapel built to house *La Moreneta* (The Black Virgin; ☯ 8-10.30am & 12.15-6.30pm Mon-Sat, 8-10.30am, 12.15-6.30pm & 7.30-8.15pm Sun & hols), a statue found nearby and venerated by hundreds of thousands of people each year. Also on the monastery site is the **Museu de Montserrat** (Plaça de Santa Maria; €5.50; ☯ 10am-6pm Mon-Fri, 10am-7pm Sat & Sun), with a varied art collection ranging from an Egyptian mummy to works by Degas and Caravaggio. Use the funiculars and walking paths to explore this incredible piece of nature.

INFORMATION
46km northwest of Barcelona
🚃 from Plaça d'Espanya & connection with *cremallera* (rack-and-pinion train) at Monistrol; 1hr; all-in-one TransMontserrat card (€20.50) includes 2 metro rides, train, *cremallera* & use of funiculars at Montserrat
ℹ️ information office (☎ 93 877 77 01)
✕ Hotel Abat Cisneros, self-service restaurants & snack bars

ORGANISED TOURS

From the excellent hop-on, hop-off bus tour of the city to walking and cycling tours, there is a broad range of opportunities to get to know the city a little better with some local help. To organise tailor-made tours, especially for groups, approach the **Barcelona Guide Bureau** (☎ 93 268 24 22; www.bgb.es).

Barri Gòtic Walking Tour

The Oficina d'Informació de Turisme de Barcelona (3, B3) organises guided walking tours of the historic heart of the city, leaving from the main tourist office on Plaça de Catalunya.
☎ **807 117222** ✉ **Plaça de Catalunya 17** € **tours €8/3** ☺ **English 10am Thu & Fri Apr-Sep, 10am Sat & Sun year-round, Spanish & Catalan noon Sat & Sun** Ⓜ **Catalunya**

Bus Turístic (5, D1) This

hop-on hop-off service runs along two circuit routes (32 stops), linking virtually all the major tourist sights. Tickets are available on the bus and each full circuit lasts about two hours.
☎ **010** ⌨ **www.tmb .net** € **day of unlimited rides €16/10, 2 consecu-tive days €20/13** ☺ **9am-7.45pm except Christmas Day & New Year's Day**

La Casa Elizalde (6, C4)

This cultural organisation organises several Barcelona walks (which generally occupy a morning and cost €5) and day or weekend excursions outside the city. Spanish and Catalan are the majority languages.
☎ **93 488 05 90** ✉ **Carrer de València 302** Ⓜ **Passeig de Gràcia**

Picasso Walking Tour

The Oficina d'Informació de Turisme de Barcelona (3, B3) organises a guided walking tour of locations in the historic heart of the city connected with the artist, including places he lived and worked. The walk takes about 1½ hours and finishes at the Museu Picasso, entry to which is included in the price.
☎ **807 117222** ✉ **Plaça de Catalunya 17** € **€10/5** ☺ **English 10.30am Sat & Sun, Spanish & Cata-lan 11.30am Sat & Sun** Ⓜ **Catalunya**

Pullmantur (4, G3)

This company runs several bus tours of Barcelona and excursions beyond. These range from half-day jaunts around the city (half/full day, including dinner in Poble Es-panyol, €34.25/89.10) to out-of-town trips to Montserrat, Girona and Figueres.
☎ **93 318 02 41** ✉ **Gran Via de les Corts Catalanes 645** Ⓜ **Girona**

Ruta del Gòtic

The Museu d'Història de la Ciutat (3, C3; p13) organises several themed walks around the old city, usually taking a couple of hours. Contact the museum for details.
☎ **93 315 11 11** ✉ **Carrer del Veguer** € **€6** Ⓜ **Jaume I**

Un Cotxe Menys (8, C3)

This bike-hire company also organises three-hour cycle tours around the Ciutat Vella, La Barce-loneta, La Sagrada Família and Port Olímpic. There is no need to book unless you are a group of 15 or more. The price includes a drink stop.
☎ **93 268 21 05** ⌨ **www.bicicletabar celona.com** ✉ **Carrer de la Espartería 3** € **€22** ☺ **10am-2pm Mon-Fri, tour 11am daily, 4.30pm Mon, Wed & Fri, 7.30pm Tue, Thu & Sat** Ⓜ **Jaume**

Shopping

It may not have been the lure of shopping that brought you to Barcelona, but it will be one of the reasons you come back. From tiny specialist stores to mammoth malls, Barcelona is a retail revelation with ample opportunity to send your bank manager into a tizzy.

Whether it's need or desire that drives your spree – or the realisation that your wardrobe is dowdy compared to that of the locals – you'll find good value and plenty of choice.

Barri Gòtic is one of the best precincts, with groovy street, club and second-hand wear shops mingling with antique and engaging junk shops. The quirky specialist stores give it a special twinkle. The boulevards of La Rambla de Catalunya and Passeig de Gràcia are lined with local and international boutiques and jewellery stores. La Ribera abounds in artisan workshops, and cool fashion can be found in El Born.

Most places have retail windows between 10am and 2pm and 4pm and 8pm. Traditional and most smaller shops observe the siesta, while the modern ones (such as fashion stores, and major book and record stores), and many on main shopping boulevards often stay open throughout the day. Department stores like El Corte Inglés and other major shops tend to open around 10am to 9pm Monday to Saturday. Virtually all shops are closed on Sunday. In July, August and in some cases September many stores adopt 'summer hours', which can mean anything but generally involves later morning starts, shorter hours and closing on Saturdays.

Tax Refunds

Visitors are entitled to a refund of the 16% sales tax (IVA) on purchases costing in excess of €90.15 if they take the goods out of the EU within three months. Ask the shop for a refund form, and then present the form (along with passport, air ticket and luggage) at customs when you depart from Spain (or elsewhere from the EU). At Barcelona airport, customs and a couple of bank branches dealing in immediate refunds are on the ground floor of terminal A.

If we just act naturally, maybe they won't find out about that great sale…

FASHION, CLOTHES & SHOES

Adolfo Domínguez (6, C5)
This Galician is one of Spain's most celebrated designers and was part of the reason the eyes of the fashion world were upon Barcelona in the early 1990s. His designs may have become a little more conservative since those heady days, but he still produces timeless fashions for men and women, with exquisite tailoring and quality materials.
☎ 93 487 41 70 🖥 www .adolfodominguez.es, in Catalan ✉ Passeig de Gràcia 32, L'Eixample ⏱ 10am-8.30pm Mon-Sat Ⓜ Passeig de Gràcia

Camper: shoes for pounding the pavement

Antonio Miró (6, B5) The doyen of Barcelona couture, Antonio Miró made his name by producing elegant and unpretentious classic fashion of the highest quality for men and women. Miró also does an attractive line in accessories.
☎ 93 487 06 70 🖥 www.antoniomiro.es ✉ Carrer del Consell de Cent 349, L'Eixample ⏱ 10am-2pm & 4.30-8.30pm Mon-Sat Ⓜ Passeig de Gràcia

Armand Basi (6, B4) Once the outfitter of James Bond, Armand Basi is a stylish stalwart. This is the only place you'll find the whole dashing collection, from classic knitwear and timeless suits to elegant evening dresses and accessories.
☎ 93 215 14 21 🖥 www.armandbasi .com ✉ Passeig de Gràcia 49, L'Eixample ⏱ 10am-9pm Mon-Sat Ⓜ Passeig de Gràcia

Bad Habits (6, C4) This is a bunker full of ballsy and original fashion for women with the confidence to take a risk. Blurring the lines between feminine and masculine, colour and monochrome, Bad Habits stocks international labels as well as its own line.
☎ 93 487 22 59 ✉ Carrer de València 261, L'Eixample ⏱ 10.30am-2.30pm & 4.30-8.30pm Mon-Sat Ⓜ Passeig de Gràcia

Camper (6, B4) This classic Mallorcan shoe merchant continues to stamp all over the international market by successfully treading the fine line between rebellion and commercialism. There are branches all over town.
☎ 93 215 63 90 🖥 www.camper.com ✉ Carrer de València 249, L'Eixample ⏱ 10am-9pm Mon-Sat Ⓜ Passeig de Gràcia

Barcelona Bargains

Serious shoppers plan their sprees around the city's seasonal sales (*rebaixes* in Catalan, *rebajas* in Castilian). Everything is marked down from the middle of January to the end of February, and summer styles are almost given away from around 5 July (sales can last well into August). It's an ideal opportunity for lucky southern-hemisphere visitors to make an absolute killing on their new wardrobe (or to second-guess next year's fashion, if you're from the northern hemisphere).

You won't just window-shop at Custo Barcelona

Custo Barcelona (8, C3)
Created in the early 1980s by the Dalmau brothers, Custo is the biggest name in contemporary Barcelona fashion and one of its trendiest exports. The company specialises in unique long-sleeved T-shirts, for men and women, with bold and psychedelic graphics. The clothes don't just jump out at you, they wrap their beautiful fabrics around your inspecting hand and lead it to your pocket. There's also a branch at Carrer de Ferran 36 (5, D4; ☎ 93 342 66 98).
☎ 93 268 78 93
🖳 www.custo-bar
celona.com ✉ Plaça de les Olles 7, La Ribera
🕑 10am-9pm Mon-Sat, noon-8pm Sun
Ⓜ Barceloneta

E-male (4, F4) If your dowdy wardrobe is holding you back on the dance floor, it may be time for a Latin make-over. This shop (and a couple of others on this street) stocks up-to-the-minute trends in international club wear, most of which require a tan and a very fit booty.
☎ 93 454 08 72
✉ Carrer del Consell de Cent 236, L'Eixample
🕑 11.30am-2pm & 5-9pm Mon-Sat
Ⓜ Universitat

Farrutx (6, A2) The splendidly sober architecture of this shop is the perfect setting to showcase the artisanal wares of one of the country's finest shoemakers, Mallorca's Farrutx, who has been expertly dressing the heels of Barcelona's uptown women for decades.
☎ 93 215 06 85
🖳 www.farrutx.com
✉ Carrer de Ros-selló 218, L'Eixample
🕑 10am-8.30pm Mon-Sat Ⓜ Diagonal

Josep Font (6, C3) One of the leading women's fash-ion designers in Barcelona (with branches in Paris, Madrid and Bilbao), Font presents a line of daringly sleek and sexy items in no-nonsense colours. The shop is worth peering into for the minimalist décor.
☎ 93 487 21 10
🖳 www.josepfont.com
✉ Carrer de Prov-ença 304, L'Eixample
🕑 10am-8.30pm Mon-Sat Ⓜ Diagonal

Mango (6, B3) Begun in Barcelona in the 1980s, Mango has gone massive around the world with its combination of sexy and sassy couture, reliable fab-rics and department-store prices. Slightly younger and funkier than its main rival, Zara (opposite), Mango produces originals as well as knock-offs from the big names. It's is a great place for fashion-savvy, budget-conscious guys and gals to stretch their euros.
☎ 93 215 75 30
🖳 www.mango.es

CLOTHING & SHOE SIZES

Women's Clothing

Aust/UK	8	10	12	14	16	18
Europe	36	38	40	42	44	46
Japan	5	7	9	11	13	15
USA	6	8	10	12	14	16

Women's Shoes

Aust/USA	5	6	7	8	9	10
Europe	35	36	37	38	39	40
France only	35	36	38	39	40	42
Japan	22	23	24	25	26	27
UK	3½	4½	5½	6½	7½	8½

Men's Clothing

Aust	92	96	100	104	108	112
Europe	46	48	50	52	54	56

Japan	S	M	M		L	
UK/USA	35	36	37	38	39	40

Men's Shirts (Collar Sizes)

Aust/Japan	38	39	40	41	42	43
Europe	38	39	40	41	42	43
UK/USA	15	15½	16	16½	17	17½

Men's Shoes

Aust/ UK	7	8	9	10	11	12
Europe	41	42	43	44½	46	47
Japan	26	27	27.5	28	29	30
USA	7½	8½	9½	10½	11½	12½

Measurements approximate only; try before you buy.

✉ Passeig de Gràcia 21, L'Eixample ◷ 10.15am-9pm Mon-Sat Ⓜ Passeig de Gràcia

Roser-Francesc (4, F3) Civilised and muted, the men's and women's collections in this store encompass a host of international labels along with local names such as Lydia Delgado, Antonio Miró and Konrad Muhr.
☎ 93 459 14 53 ✉ Carrer de València 285, L'Eixample ◷ 10.30am-2pm & 4.30-9pm Mon-Sat Ⓜ Passeig de Gràcia

Tactic (6, A5) The best shop for surf and skate wear has all the international brands you'd expect – Quiksilver, Ripcurl, Mooks, DC Shoe Co – along with a smattering of indigenous labels from around Spain.
☎ 93 451 03 87 ✉ Carrer d'Enric Granados 11, L'Eixample ◷ 5-8pm Mon, 10.45am-2pm & 5-8pm Tue-Sat Ⓜ Universitat

Zara (6, C6) The Spanish name synonymous with inexpensive and good-quality smart casuals (that aren't made in sweatshops) has blossomed internationally in recent years, thanks to a carefully commercialised fashion edge. The clothes seem more conservative in their place of origin, but you can still save a well-groomed arm and a leg by stocking up here. There are many branches around town.
☎ 93 301 09 78 ▯ www .zara.com ✉ Passeig de Gràcia 16, L'Eixample ◷ 10am-9pm Mon-Sat Ⓜ Passeig de Gràcia

Mango: always in season

DESIGN, HOMEWARE & GIFTS

Art Montfalcon (5, D3)
Beneath the over-arching vaults of this Gothic cavern is spread an incredible range of gift ideas and art. The most appealing are the prints of local and universal inspiration. Thrown in are original works of art by local artists, framed and ready to go, and a whole range of Barcelona memorabilia, from ceramics to arty T-shirts. Some of it's pure kitsch, but much of it's actually kinda classy as souvenirs go.
☎ 93 301 13 25
🖥 www.montfalcon.com
✉ Carrer dels Boters 4
🕑 10.30am-9pm Mon-Sat, 10.30am-1.30pm & 4.30-9pm Sun & hols
Ⓜ Liceu

Bd Ediciones de Diseño (4, F3) An awesome shop where you'll find classics of modern furniture design alongside bold and contemporary creations in a Modernista building constructed by Domènech i Montaner

in 1895. A must for anyone interested in design or retail atmosphere (although the prices are way out of most people's league).
☎ 93 458 69 09
🖥 www.bdbarcelona.com ✉ Carrer de Mallorca 291, L'Eixample
🕑 10am-2pm & 4-8pm Mon-Sat Ⓜ Diagonal

Dom (6, B3) Retro aesthetics are reworked in 21st-century styles at this little design shop, stacked with everyday furniture, lamps, CDs, magazines, plants, lots of things that can be inflated and far too many 'Don't Touch' signs. It has a couple of branches around town.
☎ 93 487 11 81
🖥 www.id-dom.com
✉ Carrer de Provença 249, L'Eixample
🕑 10.30am-8.30pm Mon-Fri, 10.30am-9pm Sat Ⓜ Diagonal

Dos i Una (6, B2) Fun is the watchword and style the way at this friendly

store, with all the designer accessories, gimmicks and games required to keep kids and adults entertained for hours.
☎ 93 217 70 32
✉ Carrer de Rosselló 275, L'Eixample 🕑 10.30am-2pm & 4.30-8.30pm Mon-Sat Ⓜ Diagonal

Ganiveteria Roca (5, D3)
If it needs to be cut, clipped, snipped, trimmed, shorn, shaved or cropped, you'll find the perfect instrument at this classic gentlemen's shop.
☎ 93 302 12 41
✉ Plaça del Pi 3, Barri Gòtic 🕑 9.45am-1.30pm & 4.15-8pm Mon-Fri, 10am-2pm & 5-8pm Sat Ⓜ Liceu

Marc 3 (6, B6) Step inside this cavern of posters, prints and original paintings. At the front end of the shop is a remarkably diverse range of items depicting the city you're in. A cut above the standard

Get Jeeves to pop in for a few grooming essentials at Ganiveteria Roca

in kitsch, they can make fine gifts. Deeper inside is a host of other wall-decoration ideas, from Robert Doisneau to quality reproductions of classic ad posters.
☎ 93 318 19 53 ✉ La Rambla de Catalunya 12, L'Eixample 🕐 10am-8.30pm Mon-Sat Ⓜ Catalunya

Taller de Lencería (6, B2) This is a charming little shop specialising in traditional-design bedclothes made to order and sold off the peg

with monograms embroidered while you wait.
☎ 93 415 39 52 ✉ Carrer de Rosselló 271, L'Eixample 🕐 10am-2pm & 4.30-8pm Mon-Sat Ⓜ Diagonal

Vinçon (6, B2) Despite its lofty reputation as the frame in which Spanish design evolves, this superb shop is relaxed and unpretentious. Even if you're not in the market for domestic appliances, furniture and everyday practical items, pamper

your aesthetic senses with a journey through its local and imported wares. Wander upstairs and out onto the terrace for unusual sidelong views of La Pedrera (p16). The **TincÇon** (I'm sleepy) annexe on Carrer de Rosselló 246 (6, B2) is in the same block and dedicated to – you guessed it – the bedroom.
☎ 93 215 60 50 🖥 www.vincon.com ✉ Passeig de Gràcia 96, L'Eixample 🕐 10am-8.30pm Mon-Sat Ⓜ Diagonal

FOOD & DRINK

Caelum (5, D3) From all corners of the country arrive the carefully prepared sweet goodies that have been the pride of Spanish convents through the centuries. Tempting items such as sticky marzipan (still handmade in various closed-order convents) find their way into this specialist delicacy store. Head downstairs to the cavernous café area.
☎ 93 302 69 93 ✉ Carrer de la Palla 8, Barri Gòtic 🕐 5-8.30pm Mon, 10.30am-8.30pm Tue-Thu, 10.30am-2pm Fri & Sat Ⓜ Liceu

Casa Gispert (8, B2) Nuts and coffee are roasted in an antique 19th-century wood-fired oven at this wonderfully aromatic wholesaler. Hazelnuts and almonds are the specialities, complemented by piles of dried fruit and a host of artisanal products

such as mustards and preserves.
☎ 93 319 75 35 ✉ Carrer dels Sombrerers 23, La Ribera 🕐 9.30am-1.30pm & 4-7.30pm Tue-Fri, 10am-2pm & 5-8pm Sat Ⓜ Jaume I

El Magnífico (8, A2) Take a veritable tour of world coffee with the friendly Sans family.

They had so much fun with their beans and blends that they opened another store across the street, **Sans & Sans** (8, A2; Carrer de l'Argenteria 59), devoted to more than 200 types of tea.
☎ 93 319 60 81 ✉ Carrer de l'Argenteria 64, La Ribera 🕐 9.30am-2pm & 4-8pm Mon-Fri, 9.30am-2pm Sat Ⓜ Jaume I

Nuggety Christmas Nosh
When Christmas comes, specialist pastry stores fill with *turrón*, the traditional holiday tooth-rotter. Essentially nougat, it comes in all sorts of shapes, sizes and flavours, although at the base is a sticky almond concoction. Softer blocks are known as *turrón de Valencia* and a harder version *turrón de Gijón*. Nowadays you can find it year-round, but for the best wait until Christmas and check out stores like **Planelles** (5, D1; ☎ 93 317 34 39; Av del Portal de l'Àngel 27, Barri Gòtic; 🕐 10am-10pm Mon-Sat, 4.30-9.30pm Sun & hols; metro Catalunya). It also does great ice creams and *orxata*, the summer tiger-nut drink from Valencia.

Escribà (5, C3) Chocolates, dainty pastries and mouth-watering cakes can all be lapped up behind the attractive Modernista mosaic façade here. This Barcelona favourite is owned by the Escribà family, a name synonymous with sinfully good sweet things.
☎ 93 301 60 27 ✉ La Rambla de Sant Josep 83 ◷ 8.30am-9pm Ⓜ Liceu

J Murrià (6, C3) Classic inside and out, this superb traditional-style grocer-delicatessen has been run by the same family since the early 1900s and continues to showcase the culinary wonders of Catalonia, Spain and beyond. It's a wonderful place to visit before a picnic or without excuse, and has an eye-catching façade featuring original designs by celebrated Modernista painter Ramon Casas.
☎ 93 215 57 89 ✉ Carrer de Roger de Llúria 85, L'Eixample ◷ 10am-2pm & 5-8.30pm Mon-Sat Ⓜ Passeig de Gràcia

La Portorriqueña (5, C2) Forget Starbucks, this is what coffee is supposed to be about. Beans from around the world are freshly ground before your eyes in the combination of your choice. This place has been doing this since 1902. But that's not all – it also purveys all sorts of chocolate goodies.
☎ 93 317 34 38 ✉ Carrer d'En Xuclà 25, El Raval ◷ 9am-2pm & 5-8pm Mon-Fri, 9am-2pm Sat Ⓜ Catalunya

J Murrià: a feast for the eyes and the tum

Papabubble (5, E5) Two Australians run this enchanting old-style boiled-lolly shop. With a little luck you'll wander in when they're making their sweet temptations. Otherwise, you can sample the wares and choose from classic humbugs and other multicoloured wonders, including a house speciality, life-size candy phalluses.
☎ 93 268 86 25 🖳 www.papabubble .com ✉ Carrer Ample 28 ◷ 10am-8.30pm Tue-Sun Ⓜ Drassanes

Tot Formatge (8, C2) Some gifts can be a little cheesy, and none more than the olfactory offerings in this All Cheese locale. Little platters with samples of a handful of their products are scattered about the store. In all, a powerful assembly of the best in Spanish and European cheeses is on display.
☎ 93 319 53 75 ✉ Passeig del Born 13, La Ribera ◷ 9am-2pm & 5-8pm Mon-Fri Ⓜ Jaume I

Vila Viniteca (5, F4) This unassuming little shop has a superb range of Spanish and international wines, from cheap table varieties to vintage treasures, sold by enthusiastic staff. They know their stuff, having been in the booze business since 1932.
☎ 93 268 32 27 🖳 www.vilaviniteca.es, in Castilian ✉ Carrer dels Agullers 7, La Ribera ◷ 8.30am-2.30pm & 4.30-8.30pm Mon-Sat Ⓜ Jaume I

Xampany (4, E4) Put bubbles in your basket at this atmospheric little shop lined with hundreds of varieties and brands of *cava* (Spanish sparkling wine), many of which are stocked in the original cooler from the Gran Teatre de Liceu.
☎ 610 84 50 11 ✉ Carrer de València 200, L'Eixample ◷ 10am-2pm & 4.30-7pm Tue-Fri, 4.30-7pm Mon, 10am-2pm Sat Ⓜ Hospital Clínic

BOOKS & MUSIC

Altaïr (6, B6) If you need any encouragement in planning your next trip, these travel specialists will give you a nudge in the right direction. There's knowledgeable staff, an impressive range of local-interest books, and guides and maps. Look for travel companions on the noticeboard at the front of the shop.

☎ 93 342 71 71
🖳 www.altair.es, in Castilian ✉ Gran Via de les Corts Catalanes 616, L'Eixample 🕙 10am-2pm & 4.30-8.30pm Mon-Sat 🅼 Universitat

Antinous (5, D5) An extensive bookshop with his-and-hers gay literature, Antinous is also a centre of gay culture. Out the back is a relaxed café, which doubles as an exhibition space and stage for book presentations.

☎ 93 301 90 70
🖳 www.antinouslibros .com, in Castilian ✉ Carrer de Josep Anselm Clavé 6, Barri Gòtic 🕙 9.30am-2pm & 5-8.45pm Mon-Fri, noon-2pm & 5-8.45pm Sat 🅼 Drassanes

Casa del Libro (6, C4) This chain of general bookstores is among the best-stocked in town. The Home of the Book covers a broad range of subjects and has decent sections devoted to literature in English, French and other languages. It also organises readings and book presentations.

☎ 93 272 34 80
🖳 www.casadel libro.com, in Castilian

✉ Passeig de Gràcia 62, L'Eixample 🕙 9.30am-9.30pm Mon-Sat 🅼 Passeig de Gràcia

Castelló (5, C2) This family-run chain has been tickling the earlobes of Catalans since 1935, and comprises five stores in El Raval and several others around and beyond town. Each specialises in a different genre so, between them, you're bound to hit the right chord. Aside from the main branch, you could try Carrer dels Tallers 3 (5, C2) for classical music, No 9 (5, C2) for alternative, hip-hop and other contemporary sounds and No 79 (5, B1), another general store.

☎ 93 302 59 46
🖳 www.discoscastello .es, in Castilian ✉ Carrer dels Tallers 7, El Raval 🕙 10am-8.30pm Mon-Sat 🅼 Catalunya

CD-Drome (5, C1) This excellent store has an even range of CDs and vinyl covering the main branches of dance along with one of the best indie selections in town.

☎ 93 317 46 46
✉ Carrer de Valldonzella 3, El Raval 🕙 10.30am-8pm Mon-Fri, 10.30am-2pm & 4.30-8.30pm Sat 🅼 Universitat

Come In (4, E3) If you read and think in English, this is a reasonable stop. Its strong point is teaching material, ranging from professional manuals and reference titles to readers.

☎ 93 453 12 04
✉ Carrer de Prov-ença 203, L'Eixample 🕙 9.30am-8.30pm Mon-Fri, 10.30am-2pm & 4.30-8.30pm Sat 🅼 Diagonal

Barcelona in Words

For a fascinating insight into what makes Catalonia's capital unique, there's no better read than Robert Hughes' *Barcelona*, a passionate study of the art, architecture, history and character of the city. George Orwell's first-hand account of the Spanish Civil War and its impact on Barcelona, *Homage to Catalonia*, is an enthralling examination of a tragic chapter in Spain's history, while Colm Tóibín's *Homage to Barcelona* is a wonderful anecdotal introduction to Barcelona's modern and artistic life. On a flightier note, Eduardo Mendoza's *La Ciudad de los Prodigios* (The City of Marvels) is a fantastical tale that lifts the lid on the booming Barcelona of the late 19th century. Carlos Ruiz Zafón's literary mystery, *La Sombra del Viento* (The Shadow of the Wind), is set in the Barcelona of the first half of the 20th century and was topping the bestseller charts in 2004.

Elephant (4, F5) This bright bookshop is off the main tourist tracks but is a helpful haven of books in the Queen's English. Stock ranges from fiction to kids' stuff, with a smattering of reference works and a healthy second-hand section.
☎ 93 443 05 94 ⊠ **Carrer de la Creu dels Molers 12, Poble Sec** ☽ **10am-8pm Mon-Sat** Ⓜ **Poble Sec**

Etnomusic (5, C2) From flamenco to samba and whatever jiggles in between, this is your best bet for music from around the globe.
☎ 93 301 18 84 🖳 **www.etnomusic.com** ⊠ **Carrer del Bonsuccès 6, El Raval**

☽ **11am-2pm & 5-8pm Mon-Sat** Ⓜ **Catalunya**

Laie (6, C6) A leisure complex for the mind, this bookshop combines a broad range of books with a splendid café (☽ 9am-9pm Mon, 9am-1am Tue-Sat), an international outlook and accommodating staff.
☎ 93 318 17 39 🖳 **www.laie.es, in Castilian & Catalan** ⊠ **Carrer de Pau Claris 85, L'Eixample** ☽ **10am-9pm Mon-Fri, 10.30am-9pm Sat** Ⓜ **Urquinaona**

Próleg (3, C3) More like a club than a bookshop, this store is run by women for women and concentrates on

---

feminist titles. It also organises activities such as writing workshops and forums.
☎ 93 319 24 25 🖳 **www.mallorcaweb .net/proleg** ⊠ **Carrer de la Dagueria 13, Barri Gòtic** ☽ **5-8pm Mon, 10am-2pm & 5-8pm Tue-Fri, 11am-2pm & 5-8pm Sat** Ⓜ **Jaume I**

Wah Wah (5, B3) Best on a street with lots of decent music shops, Wah Wah is chock-full of 1970s vinyl but also has good techno stock.
☎ 93 442 37 03 ⊠ **Carrer de la Riera Baixa 14, El Raval** ☽ **11am-2pm & 5-8.30pm Mon-Sat** Ⓜ **Sant Antoni or Liceu**

ANTIQUES & CRAFTS

Bulevard dels Antiquaris (6, B4) Part of the Bulevard Rosa shopping mall, this stretch is crammed with more than 70 antique shops tempting you with the this-and-that of old. A few specialists to look out for include Brahuer (jewellery), Trik-Trak (old tin toys), Govary's (porcelain dolls), Dalmau (wooden picture frames) and Victory (crystal).
☎ 93 215 44 99 ⊠ **Passeig de Gràcia 55, L'Eixample** ☽ **10.30am-2pm & 5-8.30pm Mon-Sat** Ⓜ **Passeig de Gràcia**

Gemma Povo (5, D3) Several streets in the heart of old Barcelona bustle with decades of collected furniture, gewgaws and other odd sights. Rummagers should head for Carrer de la Palla

---

and Carrer dels Nous Banys for starters. In the latter is this interesting stop, where alongside quality furniture you'll find items in the house speciality: wrought iron.
☎ 93 301 34 76 ⊠ **Carrer dels Banys Nous 5-7, Barri Gòtic** ☽ **10am-1.30pm & 4.30-8pm** Ⓜ **Liceu**

Germanes García (5, D3) Welcome to the wonderful world of wicker. This vast, rambling store has anything you could want in the stuff, from chairs and clothes baskets to model trains. You may not want to buy, but it's an extraordinary place to browse.
☎ 93 318 66 46 ⊠ **Carrer dels Banys Nous 15** ☽ **4.30-7.30pm Mon, 9.30am-1.30pm & 4.30-7.30pm Tue-Sat** Ⓜ **Liceu**

Gotham (5, E4) This great retro shop specialises in furniture and furnishings from the 1950s, '60s and '70s but you'll also find a mix of older stuff and up-to-the-minute new designs – a curious all-sorts mix.
☎ 93 412 46 47 ⊠ **Carrer de Cervantes 7, Barri Gòtic** ☽ **10.30am-2pm & 5-8.30pm Mon-Sat** Ⓜ **Jaume I**

Gothsland Galeria d'Art (6, B5) They're probably not the take-home variety of antiques, but this place stocks a unique collection of furniture, art and decorations, some of a Modernista ilk.
☎ 93 488 19 22 ⊠ **Carrer del Consell de Cent 331, L'Eixample** ☽ **10am-2pm & 4.30-8.30pm Mon-Sat** Ⓜ **Passeig de Gràcia**

DEPARTMENT STORES & MALLS

Bulevard Rosa (6, B4)
With over 100 shops featuring some of the most interesting local designers of fashion and jewellery, this 1980s creation is the best mall in the city for style and a few hours of boutique-browsing.
☎ 93 215 83 31
🖳 www.bulevardrosa .com ✉ Passeig de Gràcia 55-57, L'Eixample ⏱ 10.30am-8.30pm Mon-Sat Ⓜ Passeig de Gràcia

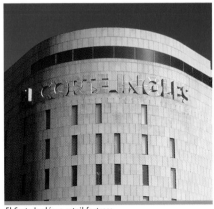
El Corte Inglés: a retail fortress

El Corte Inglés (5, E1)
This monster of retail has everything you could possibly want and lots more that won't have crossed your mind. There's also a rooftop café with a splendid view. There are branches around the city at Avda Diagonal 471 (4, D3; ☎ 93 493 48 00), Avda Diagonal 617 (4, C4; ☎ 93 367 71 00) and Avda del Portal de l'Àngel 19 (5, D2; ☎ 93 306 38 00).
☎ 93 306 38 00
🖳 www.elcorteingles.es, in Castilian ✉ Plaça de Catalunya 14, L'Eixample ⏱ 10am-10pm Mon-Sat Ⓜ Catalunya

El Triangle (5, D1)
Occupying an entire corner of Plaça de Catalunya, this modern mall can seem lacking in style for such a strategic location, but it's redeemed by some worthy stores including FNAC and Sephora (p62).
☎ 93 318 01 08
✉ Plaça de Catalunya 4, L'Eixample ⏱ 10am-10pm Mon-Sat Ⓜ Catalunya

FNAC (5, D1) This popular
megastore – part of the French-owned chain – specialises in CDs, tapes, videos, books and video games. There's a useful ticket desk on the ground floor, which has lists of upcoming events and sells tickets.
☎ 93 344 18 00
🖳 www.fnac.es, in Castilian ✉ El Triangle, Plaça de Catalunya 4, L'Eixample ⏱ 10am-10pm Mon-Sat Ⓜ Catalunya

L'Illa del Diagonal (4, C3)
This massive shopping centre in the heart of the business district caters to uptowners and houses swanky designer stores and all the usual chains. In its heyday it was acclaimed for its architectural style, and as shopping centres go it is one of the more appealing.
☎ 93 444 00 00
🖳 www.lilla.com ✉ Avda Diagonal 545, L'Eixample ⏱ 10am-9.30pm Mon-Sat Ⓜ Maria Cristina

Take a Spin on the Shopping Bus
The T1 Tombbús route was set up for shoppers and runs from Plaça de Catalunya up along Avda Diagonal, taking in many department stores and the more mainstream shopping precincts. It operates from 8am to 9.30pm Monday to Saturday and costs €1.25. (The name means 'circle bus' and isn't necessarily an invitation to retail yourself into an early grave.)

JEWELLERY, PERFUME & ACCESSORIES

Bagués (5, C3) This is more than just any old jewellery store. The boys from Bagués have been chipping away at precious stones and moulding metal since the 19th century, and many of their classic pieces have a flighty Modernista influence. They have a branch in Casa Amatller (p39).
☎ 93 318 38 42 ✉ La Rambla de Sant Josep 105 ◷ 10am-2pm & 4.30-8pm Mon-Fri, 11am-2pm Sat Ⓜ Liceu

Collector's Corner (3, C3) This cute shop is a veritable Aladdin's cave for fans of fragrance. Along with a dazzling display of ornamental miniatures, you'll find promotional cards, jewellery, powders, beads and everything else that tells a story from the history of perfume. Ask to see the albums of original labels from French companies of the 1920s and '30s that are too precious to display.
☎ 93 315 11 05 ▣ www.perfumecol.com ✉ Baixada de la Llibreteria 8, Barri Gòtic ◷ 5-8pm Mon-Sat Ⓜ Jaume I

Forvm Ferlandina (5, B2) Contemporary jewellery from local designers and European names in everything from plastic to platinum can be found at this shop, which also hosts exhibitions by leading jewellers.
☎ 93 441 80 18 ▣ www.forvmjoies.com ✉ Carrer de Ferlandina 31, El Raval ◷ 11am-2pm & 5-8.30pm Tue-Fri, 11am-2pm Sat Ⓜ Universitat

Joaquín Berao (6, B4) For something very special, head to this elegant store showcasing the exquisite avant-garde creations of one of Spain's most prestigious designers. He works predominantly in silver and gold, and with new and entirely original concepts each season.
☎ 93 215 00 91 ▣ www.joaquinberao.com ✉ La Rambla de Catalunya 74, L'Eixample ◷ 10am-2pm & 5-8.30pm Mon-Sat Ⓜ Passeig de Gràcia

Loewe (6, B5) In his guide, *Barcelona*, international art critic Robert Hughes urges anyone with an interest in architecture not to patronise Loewe because of the vandalism it inflicted on this Domènech i Montaner Modernista building. If you're prepared to forgive the company – and it has tried to atone for its sin – Loewe is one of the smartest international names in luxurious leather products.
☎ 93 216 04 00 ▣ www.loewe.com ✉ Passeig de Gràcia 35, L'Eixample ◷ 10am-8.30pm Mon-Sat Ⓜ Passeig de Gràcia

Sephora (5, C1) This zebra-striped temple of fragrance is the largest in Europe and has every scent you've ever heard of, along with local flavours by the likes of Antonio Miró and Jesús Del Pozo. A perfume organ allows you to experiment with your perfect eau, and if you don't come up smelling of roses, they'll happily exchange your fragrance.
☎ 93 306 39 00 ✉ El Triangle, Carrer de Pelai 13-39, L'Eixample ◷ 10am-10pm Mon-Sat Ⓜ Catalunya

You'll leave a scented trail after you visit Sephora

MARKETS

Market Squares

Make the most of Barcelona's many markets:

- **Plaça Nova** (3, A1) Antiques and bric-a-brac on Thursday
- **Plaça de Sant Josep Oriol** (5, D3) Arts and crafts on Saturday and Sunday
- **Plaça del Pi** (5, D3) Artisanal food products Friday to Sunday every fortnight
- **Plaça Reial** (5, D4) Stamps and coins on Sunday morning
- **Mercat de Sant Antoni** (4, F5) Old maps, stamps, books and cards on Sunday morning

Els Encants Vells (4, H2)
Barcelona's biggest and most authentic flea market is 'The Old Charms', where bargain-hunters riffle through every-thing from battered old shoes and bric-a-brac to antique furniture and new clothes. A lot of it is junk, but it depends on what's fallen off trucks the day you turn up.
☎ 93 246 30 30
✉ Carrer del Dos de Maig (cnr of Plaça de les Glòries Catalanes), L'Eixample ⏱ 8am-7pm Mon, Wed, Fri & Sat (best choice in the morning) Ⓜ Glòries

Mercat de la Boqueria (5, C3) One of Europe's best and most famous markets, this bustling produce hall is laden with atmosphere, colour and all the ingredients that make Spanish cuisine a favourite at the kitchen table. You'll find fresh food of all types here, and it's a wonderful place to wander and just follow your nose, especially in the morning, when it's not full of tourists.
☎ 93 318 25 84
✉ La Rambla de Sant Josep 91 ⏱ 8am-8.30pm Mon-Sat Ⓜ Liceu

Is that an unframed Picasso? You never know what you might find at Els Encants Vells...

FOR CHILDREN

Cuca Fera (8, B1) Original retro clobber from the 1960s and '70s for newborns to eight-year-olds can be found at this charismatic treasure trove near El Born.
☎ 93 268 37 10 ✉ Carrer de Cremat Gran 9, La Ribera 🕑 10am-2pm & 5-9pm Mon-Fri, 10am-3pm & 4-9pm Sat Ⓜ Jaume I

Du Pareil au Même (6, A3) Barcelona's only outlet of this French chain stocks fun, durable and colourful clothes designed to be worn in layers by boys and girls from three months to 12 years old.
☎ 93 287 14 49 ✉ La Rambla de Catalunya 95, L'Eixample 🕑 10am-8.30pm Mon-Sat Ⓜ Diagonal

Joguines Foyè (5, D3) The best toy shop in the old quarter stocks lots of traditional playthings such as tin toys, creepy porcelain dolls and music boxes as well as a range of modern gizmos.
☎ 93 302 03 89 ✉ Carrer dels Banys Nous 13, Barri Gòtic 🕑 10am-2pm & 4.30-8pm Mon-Fri,

10am-2pm & 5-8pm Sat Ⓜ Liceu

Mullor (6, A3) Exquisite traditional dresses and suits for newborns to four-year-olds come from this Catalan family business, which has been making clothes in linen, wool, cotton and silk to the same designs for the last 50 years. It specialises in cherubic christening outfits and formal gear.
☎ 93 488 09 02 ✉ La Rambla de Catalunya 102, L'Eixample 🕑 10.30am-2pm & 4.30-8.15pm Mon-Sat Ⓜ Passeig de Gràcia

SPECIALIST STORES

Arlequí Màscares (8, A1) A little house of horrors (or delights, depending on your mood), this shop specialises in masks to wear and for decoration. Stock also includes a beautiful range of decorative boxes in Catalan themes.
☎ 93 268 27 52 🖥 www.arlequimask.com ✉ Carrer de la Princesa 7, La Ribera 🕑 10.30am-8pm Mon-Sat, 10.30am-4pm Sun Ⓜ Jaume I

Cereria Subirà (3, C3) Even if you're not interested in flickering flames, you'll be impressed by the ornate décor here. Nobody can hold a candle to these people in terms of longevity – the Subirà name in wax and wicks has been in demand since 1761, although it's only been at

this address since late in the 19th century.
☎ 93 315 26 06 ✉ Baixada de la Llibreteria 7, Barri Gòtic 🕑 9am-1.30pm & 4-7.30pm Mon-Fri, 9am-1.30pm Sat Ⓜ Jaume I

Drap (5, D3) This busy shop brings out the giddy little girl in all of us – which generally comes as a surprise to blokes – as it's packed to the rafters with everything relating to dolls and their wellbeing, from miniature jars of jam to intricate handmade mansions.
☎ 93 318 14 87 ✉ Carrer del Pi 14, Barri Gòtic 🕑 10am-1.30pm & 4.30-8.30pm Mon-Fri, 10am-1.30pm & 5-8.45pm Sat Ⓜ Liceu

El Ingenio (5, D4) A bewildering range of tricks, fancy dress, masks and other

accessories to liven up your party. Here's where you can get your stick-on Salvador Dalí moustache and go around telling everyone that the moon is made of cheese.
☎ 93 317 71 38 ✉ Carrer d'En Rauric 6, Barri Gòtic 🕑 10.30am-2pm & 4.15-8pm Mon-Sat Ⓜ Liceu

La Condoneria (5, D3) Spaniards call them *consoladores*, a much nicer word than dildos. If you've left yours at home, this is a cheerful and utterly untacky spot to find a replacement. While you're at it, stock up on orange-scented lube and perhaps a packet of lurid green ribbed condoms.
☎ 93 302 77 21 🖥 www.lacondoneria.com, in Castilian ✉ Plaça de Sant Josep Oriol 3, Barri Gòtic 🕑 10.30am-2pm & 4-8.30pm Mon-Sat Ⓜ Liceu

**L'Estanc de Laietana
(5, F4)** The place where
cigar smokers come to feel
loved, the entire shop is
a humidor and stocks the
best cigars from around the
world, along with hundreds
of brands of cigarettes and
rolling tobacco.
☎ 93 310 10 34 ✉ Via
Laietana 4, La Ribera
🕑 9am-2pm & 4-7.30pm
Mon-Fri, 10am-2pm Sat
Ⓜ Jaume I

**L'Herboristeria del Rei
(5, D4)** This soothing
shop is framed by a grand
balcony and lined with
the tiny drawers of herbal
specimens that have kept it
in business since 1823. The
shop took the name when
it became court herbalist
to Queen Isabel II (but
changed it pretty swiftly
during the two Republican
periods).
☎ 93 318 05 12
✉ Carrer de Vidre 1,
Barri Gòtic 🕑 5-8pm
Mon, 10am-2pm & 5-8pm
Tue-Sat Ⓜ Liceu

Norma Comics (5, H1)
The largest comic store in
the city (indeed the biggest
comic store chain in Europe)
has a comic gallery, an
astonishing international
collection that stretches
from *Batman* and *Tintin*
through to Manga comics
and the more-or-less porn
items such as *Kiss*. Apart
from the latter two, there's
plenty for kids of all ages,
including a range of toy
superheroes and monsters.
☎ 93 244 84 23
🖵 www.norma-ed.es, in
Castilian ✉ Passeig de
Sant Joan 7-9, L'Eixample
🕑 10.30am-2pm &
5-8.30pm Mon-Thu,
10.30am-8.30pm Fri & Sat
Ⓜ Arc de Triomf

Obach (5, D4) If the hat
ever makes a comeback,
the Obach family of
milliners, in the heart of
what was once the Jew-
ish quarter (or Call) of
medieval Barcelona, stands
to make a killing. Since
1924 it has been providing
gentlemen with apparel for
their scones.
☎ 93 318 40 94 ✉ Car-
rer del Call 2, Barri Gòtic
🕑 9.30am-2pm & 4-8pm
Mon-Fri, 10am-2pm &
4.30-8pm Sat Ⓜ Liceu

Sestienda (5, D4) An
exclusively gay sex shop
where you can get your gay
map of the city along with
all the apparatus required
for a happy holiday. It's
been in business since
1981 and was the first of
its kind in Spain, then only
beginning to truly stretch
its democratic muscles
after decades of Franco's
oppression.
☎ 93 318 86 76
🖵 www.sestienda.com,
in Castilian ✉ Carrer
d'En Rauric 11, Barri Gòtic
🕑 10am-8.30pm Mon-
Sat Ⓜ Liceu

WORKcenter (5, F1) Need
a late-night photocopy? Or
fancy a quick spin on the
Web at some ungodly hour?
This could be the place for
you. Night owls and hard
workers come in for those
last-minute jobs at any
time of the day or night.
There are several branches
around town.
☎ 902 115011
🖵 www.workcenter
direct.com ✉ Carrer
de Roger de Llúria 2,
L'Eixample 🕑 24 hr
Ⓜ Urquinaona

Pearls & Swirls

Although fashion icons such as Zara and Mango have probably overtaken them
in the global shopper's consciousness, for a long time the biggest international
names in Spanish retail were **Majorica** (www.majorica.com, in Castilian), for
pearls, and **Lladró** (www.lladro.com), for porcelain. Although Majorica's head
office is in Barcelona, its factories are based in Mallorca, where pearls are arti-
ficially created for export. Majorica's collections come in all sorts of colours and
sizes. For decorating mantelpieces rather than necks, Lladró is a maker of classic
ceramic figurines and collectibles. You can find samples of both in selected stores,
including branches of El Corte Inglés department stores. Or, for porcelain pieces,
try **Lladró** (6, C6; ☎ 93 270 12 53; Passeig de Gràcia 11; 🕑 10am-8.30pm;
metro Catalunya)

Eating

No matter what your budget, taste or belly size, you'll find something to suit in Barcelona. It teems with cafés and restaurants dishing up everything from tiny tapas to gargantuan feasts.

A few old-guard restaurants specialise in traditional Catalan cooking, while other equally venerable establishments, often run by Basques or Galicians, offer a mix of their regional specialities and what can be loosely termed 'Spanish cooking'. Such places are scattered across the Barri Gòtic, El Raval and L'Eixample. Seafood is also prominent, especially in La Barceloneta.

Tapas are not a Catalan tradition but internal migration has long made them part of the local scene. The Basque version (better known as *pintxos* or *montaditos* and more like small *canapés*) are particularly popular.

Since the mid-1990s there has been a cuisine revolution in Barcelona. Inspired by guru Ferran Adriá (whose El Bulli restaurant on the north Catalan coast has become a beacon for European gourmets), a phalanx of innovative chefs is inundating the city with avant-garde cooking. Foreign cuisines are also taking off.

When it's warm, Barcelonins like to eat outside at *terrazas* (pavement tables). About the only downside is that few places are far from the rumble of traffic.

A fine Catalan institution is the *granja* (dairy bar), where you can indulge in pastries and sweet milky pick-me-ups at any time of the day – look out for the sticky thick chocolate beverages.

> ## El Compte, Sisplau (The Bill, Please)
> The price ranges used here indicate the cost per person of a full meal (starter, main and dessert), including a bottle of modest wine:
>
> | | |
> |---|---|
> | $ | up to €15 |
> | $$ | €16-29 |
> | $$$ | €30-50 |
> | $$$$ | over €50 |

Dining Hours & Booking

Catalans eat late and, often, they eat big: most have three or even four courses for lunch (between 2pm and 4pm), and nobody sits down for dinner much before 9.30pm. Most places have a day or two off, frequently Sunday or Monday, and many close for a few weeks in August. In this chapter, we have indicated whether places are open for lunch & dinner, lunch only or dinner only, and their opening days if they're not open all week. Full opening times are given for places whose mealtime hours differ greatly from the norm outlined here.

Booking is advisable at mid-range and expensive places, especially Thursday to Saturday.

Catalan Cuisine

Catalonia has a reputation for producing some of Spain's finest cuisine. It's not just a matter of a few regional dishes but a gastronomy distinct from that found elsewhere in the country or in neighbouring France. A geographically diverse region, Catalonia produces a variety of fresh, high-quality seafood, meat, poultry, game, fruit and vegetables. These can come in unusual combinations: meat and seafood (a genre known as *mar i muntanya* – the local equivalent of surf 'n' turf), poultry and fruit, fish and nuts.

Catalans find it hard to understand why other people put butter on bread when *pa amb tomàquet* – toasted or grilled bread slices rubbed with tomato, olive oil, garlic and salt – is so much tastier.

Pernil (ham) and *formatge* (cheese) are culinary constants. The main centres of cheese production in Catalonia are in La Seu d'Urgell, the Cerdanya district and the Pallars area in the northwest. Although many traditional cheeses are disappearing, you'll still be able to find things such as *formatge de tupí*, a goat's cheese soaked in olive oil, and *gorritxa*, another goat's cheese (made with penicillium mould) that is meltingly soft on the tongue. You'll also find all sorts of sausages, using pork as a base. Some generic names include *botifarra*, *fuet* (a thin, dried pork sausage) and *llonganissa*.

Catalans are passionate about *bolets* (wild mushrooms), often disappearing for days in autumn to pick them, and *calçots* (large sweet spring onions), which are roasted over hot coals, dipped in spicy *romesco* sauce (a finely ground mixture of tomatoes, peppers, onions, garlic, almonds and olive oil) and eaten voraciously when in season from January until March.

In Catalan kitchens, greater importance is attributed to sauces than in much of the rest of Spain. The most common are *sofregit* (fried onion, tomato and garlic), *samfaina* (similar to ratatouille – *sofregit* plus red pepper and aubergine or courgette), *allioli* (pounded garlic with olive oil, often with egg yolk added to make it more of a mayonnaise) and *picada* (based on ground almonds and other ingredients, such as garlic, parsley, nuts and breadcrumbs, to suit each dish).

Rice is grown in the Delta de l'Ebre area in southern Catalonia and put to a variety of good uses. *Arròs a la cassola* or *arròs a la catalana* is Catalan paella, cooked in an earthenware pot and without saffron, whereas *arròs negre* is rice cooked in cuttlefish ink – it's much tastier than it sounds. Another speciality is *fideuá*, which is similar to paella but uses vermicelli noodles rather than rice as the base. You should also receive a little side dish of *allioli* to mix in as you wish – if you don't, ask for it.

The Catalan version of the pizza is the *coca*. There are many variations, both savoury and sweet. The savoury option can come with tomato, onion, pepper and sometimes sardines. The sweet version, generally almond-based, is more common and is a standard item at many a *festa* (festival) throughout the year.

Traditional desserts include *crema Catalana*, a delicious version of *crème brûlée*, but you might also be offered *mel i mató*, honey and fresh cream cheese. Another alternative is the appealingly named *music* – dried fruits and nuts, sometimes mixed with ice cream or cream cheese, and served with a glass of sweet muscatel wine.

LA RAMBLA

The terrace restaurants on La Rambla are all much of an overpriced muchness. You won't find anywhere particularly good for dinner, but the tables are good for a sip and a snack and provide front-row seats for the show.

Attic (5, D2) $$
International
You'll find it hard to believe that this was once a cut-price supermarket. Now it's one of the few seriously inviting eateries along this open-24-hours concourse. Shimmy upstairs and try to grab a Rambla-side table for a broad mix of reasonable international food, anything from a nice beef fillet to Asia-Med mixes with rice.
☎ 93 302 48 66
✉ **La Rambla dels Estudis 120** ☾ **lunch & dinner**
Ⓜ **Catalunya, Liceu**

Start Your Day the Catalan Way

A coffee and *pasta* (pastry) is the typical breakfast in Barcelona, although in a few places (generally known as *churrerías*) you can also find the more quintessentially Spanish favourite of *churros con chocolate* (a deep-fried pastry dunked in a thick hot chocolate beverage). Other popular options include *torrades/tostadas* (toast accompanied by anything from butter to jam or honey) and the ubiquitous *bikini* (*sandwich mixto* to other Spaniards), a toasted ham-and-cheese sandwich. Freshly squeezed *suc de taronja* (orange juice; *zumo de naranja* in Castilian) is a frequent accompaniment.

Café de l'Òpera (5, D4) $
Café
Opposite the Gran Teatre del Liceu (p38), this busy cafè is easily the most atmospheric, having stood the test of time. It'll probably still be going when the nearby McDonald's and Irish pubs have all long gone. Bohemians and their buddies mingle with tourists beneath Art Deco images of opera heroines etched into mirrors. The snacks are so-so, and the waiters are marvellously unfussed. The rear end of the ground floor exudes a rambunctious bonhomie, while upstairs (get a window seat) the air is rather more hushed.
☎ 93 317 75 85
✉ **La Rambla 74**
☾ **9am-midnight**
Ⓜ **Liceu**

Cafè Zurich (5, D1) $
Café
The original 1920s Cafè Zurich was one of the city's landmark meeting places but was torn down in 1997 to make way for the department store that now occupies this corner. Its shiny, pseudoclassic replacement may not have the same charm, but it still has perfectly positioned tables for watching the world go by.
☎ 93 317 91 53
✉ **Carrer de Pelai 39**
☾ **9am-midnight**
Ⓜ **Catalunya**

BARRI GÒTIC

Agut (5, E5) $$
Catalan

This warm, friendly family-run restaurant appeals to a sedate, mature crowd that digs its traditional and robust Catalan fare. If you order a fillet of beef, that's exactly what you'll get, so ask for veggies if you require frills.
☎ 93 315 17 09
✉ Carrer d'En Gignàs 16
🕙 lunch & dinner Tue-Sat, lunch Sun Ⓜ Jaume I

Bagel Shop (5, D2) $
Snacks

When you need a break from rich Catalan food, check out this bright and chirpy neighbourhood joint, with its tasty and innovative bagels and toppings, and soups, salads and sweets. It's also handy for a picnic shop, and you can buy your doughy rings by the armful.
☎ 93 302 41 61
✉ Carrer de la Canuda 25
🕙 9.30am-9.30pm Mon-Sat, 11am-4pm Sun
Ⓜ Catalunya

Bar Celta (5, E5) $
Galician tapas

The stormy Atlantic in Spain's northwest throws up all sorts of seafood goodies that wind up in bars like this as tapas. *Pulpo a la gallega* is one – chunks of boiled octopus in a slightly spicy oil mix. Accompany with *pimientos de Padrón* (Galician peppers, some of which are hot and others not – you only find out when it's too late) and a shallow cup of crisp Ribeiro white.
☎ 93 315 00 06
✉ Carrer de la Mercè 16

Vegetarian Options

Despite the (un)popular myth, Barcelona needn't mean *tortilla* tedium for vegetarians. Along with reasonable meat-free restaurants such as **Organic** (p75), **Biocenter** (p73), **L'Atzavara** (p78) and **Comme-Bio** (p76), you'll find choice and flavour at **La Flauta Màgica** (p77), **La Cereria** (p70) and **Maoz** (p71).

Look for Ⓥ – it indicates that the place concerned is either fully vegetarian or has a good selection of vegetarian dishes.

🕙 noon-midnight
Ⓜ Drassanes

Cafè de l'Acadèmia (5, E4) $$
Catalan

An old favourite with hungry, hard-working public servants in the nearby Ajuntament, this café never fails to satisfy the demands of its loyal punters. The key to its success is a solid grounding in well-prepared local cuisine with the occasional inventive twist. The atmosphere hums good-naturedly at lunchtime but is rather more subdued and romantic in the evening.
☎ 93 319 82 53 ✉ Carrer de Lledó 1 🕙 lunch & dinner Mon-Fri Ⓜ Jaume I

Can Culleretes (5, D4) $$
Catalan

Barcelona's oldest restaurant (it was founded in 1786)

is still going strong, with tourists and locals flocking to enjoy its rambling interior, old-fashioned décor, and enormous helpings of traditional Catalan food. If the wild-boar stew doesn't grab you, try the lighter seafood options. Service with a snarl is compensated for by the timeless setting.
☎ 93 317 30 22
✉ Carrer d'En Quintana 5
🕙 lunch & dinner Tue-Sat, lunch Sun
Ⓜ Liceu

Cometacinc (5, E4) $$
Fusion

This fabulously atmospheric medieval den turns out an ever-changing menu of items that transgress all culinary boundaries. Salads come in all sorts of unexpected mixes, or you could opt for a pseudo-Thai dish.

The candle-lit tables over two floors add a touch of cosy mysteriousness.
☎ 93 310 15 58 ✉ Carrer del Cometa 5 ☽ dinner Wed-Mon Ⓜ Jaume I

El Paraguayo (5, D6) $$
South American
Forget Catalan refinements, teasing tapas or avant-garde pretensions. Here the word is meat – juicy slabs of the stuff. You can tuck into all sorts of tasty cuts of beef, pork and other flesh in this little Latin American oasis. Try the *entraña*; the word means 'entrails', but the meal is in fact a juicy slice of prime beef folded over onto itself and accompanied by a herb sauce.
☎ 93 302 14 41 ✉ Carrer del Parc 1 ☽ lunch & dinner Tue-Sun Ⓜ Drassanes

Els Quatre Gats (5, E2) $$$
Catalan
A former artists' lair where Picasso had his first exhibition, 'the four cats' (Catalan slang for 'a few people') became a legendary base for the Modernisme movement. It now has a smart café with reproductions of the original art and décor (and a huge list of beers), as well as an atmospheric restaurant out the back. Take a ground-floor seat and gaze around the mezzanine galleries.
☎ 93 302 41 40 ✉ Carrer de Montsió 3 bis ☽ 1pm-1am Ⓜ Catalunya

Granja Dulcinea (5, D3) $
Dairy Bar
Possibly Barcelona's best-known dairy bar is the perfect place to indulge in sweet, frothy delights such as a *suís* (chocolate with lashings of whipped cream) and to dip *melindros* (soft sugar-coated biscuits) into *cacaolat* (chocolate) so thick that you drink it with a spoon, all served by bow-tied waiters. Salvador Dalí used to pop in here when in town.
☎ 93 302 68 24 ✉ Carrer de Petritxol 2 ☽ 9am-1pm & 5-9pm Ⓜ Liceu ♿

La Cereria (5, D4) $
Café
Far from the bum-bags and camcorders, yet in the heart of the Barri Gòtic, this co-operative is a terrific place to chill out, surrounded by young Barcelonins filling the colourful room with smoke and bonhomie. On offer are tasty (mainly) vegetarian dishes such as *bocadillos* (filled rolls), home-made desserts, fruit shakes and fragrant teas.
☎ 93 301 85 10 ✉ Baixada de Sant Miquel 3-5 ☽ 10.30am-11.30pm Ⓜ Liceu Ⓥ

Los Caracoles (5, D5) $$$
Catalan
This 19th-century tavern is the Barri Gòtic's most

Art, history, a great range of beers – just a few reasons to visit Els Quatre Gats

picturesque restaurant and is famous for its spit-roasted chickens and, as the name suggests, snails. These days it's frequented by tourists rather than the celebrities whose photos adorn its walls, and the food is not world-class. However, when it comes to atmosphere and fairly decent snails, it still has something going for it.

☎ 93 302 31 85
✉ **Carrer dels Escudellers 14** 🕑 **lunch & dinner**
Ⓜ **Drassanes**

Maoz (5, D4) $
Middle Eastern
Shake your falafel to this Israeli joint, which attracts constant queues of students, travellers, blue-collar workers and beggars. The drawcard is the limitless salad buffet from which you choose abundant fillings to add to the basic deep-fried chickpea balls. With some judicious stacking, your snack will bulge and keep hunger pangs at bay until dinner. The formula is so successful that other branches are appearing around town.

✉ **Carrer de Ferran 13**
🕑 **noon-2am**
Ⓜ **Liceu** Ⓥ

Snails? They taste like chicken…Los Caracoles (opposite)

Margarita Blue (5, D5) $$
Mexican
Before you do anything else, sidle up to the bar for a long margarita. This place is lively, loud and hip, and will put you in the mood for some cheery Mexican nosh, which you can enjoy at tables at the back of the long bar area. The food is surprisingly creative and satisfying, and it isn't unkind on the hips.

☎ 93 317 71 76
✉ **Carrer de Josep Anselm Clavé 6** 🕑 **lunch & dinner** Ⓜ **Drassanes**

Ménage à Trois (5, D2) $$
Mediterranean
This groovy place provides an unceasingly cool terrace for summer chillin'. Adventurous cooking puts creative twists on classic themes (how about a little beef daubed in a honey-and-Baileys mix?) without pretension, and there are some vegetarian specials. Check out the art on the walls.

☎ 93 301 55 42
✉ **Carrer d'En Bot 4**
🕑 **lunch & dinner Mon-Sat, dinner Sun**
Ⓜ **Liceu** Ⓥ

Menú del Día
Virtually every restaurant in Barcelona has a set lunch menu (*menú del día*, or meal of the day), which consists of three courses and a drink. The meals cost about half as much (and sometimes less still) as ordering à la carte and provide the perfect opportunity for you to sample food from restaurants that might otherwise be beyond your fiscal comfort zone.

Mesón del Café (3, B3) $

Café

Cramped or cosy depending on your mood, this charming café is the ideal spot to while away a rainy afternoon or take the weight off any old time. Your entertaining host likes nothing more than engaging in some friendly pidgin banter with the passing trade. A satisfying morning cup of hot chocolate with *churros* will cost you €2.50.

☎ 93 315 07 54
✉ Carrer de la Llibreteria 16 ⏲ 7.30am-10.30pm Mon-Sat Ⓜ Jaume I

Philippus (5, D3) $

Café

You will be drawn in beneath broad, centuries-old stone arches for a long breakfast or to taste anything from the range of teas to the array of foreign beers. A tempting display of pastries awaits

---

Out to Lunch with the Kids

Kids are welcome at most restaurants, although it's rare to find special menus, children's portions and high chairs. Look for the Ⓕ listed with individual reviews for places where you are most likely to feel at home while chowing down with your little travellers.

---

in this former 18th-century church oratory.

☎ 93 342 64 81
✉ Carrer de la Palla 10
⏲ 10am-9pm
Ⓜ Liceu Ⓕ

Pla (5, E4) $$$

Mediterranean

The chicest choice in the Gothic quarter, this place has black-and-white menus featuring photographs of staff in action, mainly serving superb and innovative modern Mediterranean dishes with Asian twists, and making guests feel warmly welcome.

☎ 93 412 65 52 ✉ Carrer de Bellafila 5 ⏲ lunch & dinner Ⓜ Jaume I

Restaurant Pitarra (5, E5) $$$

Catalan

This restaurant, established in 1890, occupies the house where the 19th-century playwright Serafí Pitarra penned most of his work. The walls are crammed with old art, and the food is traditional Catalan. If the splayed pig with half his hindquarters carved off doesn't grab you, try out some of the hearty meat dishes.

☎ 93 301 16 47
✉ Carrer d'Avinyó 56
⏲ lunch & dinner
Mon-Sat Ⓜ Drassanes

Shunka (5, E2) $$$

Japanese

In the first years of the present millennium, Japanese restaurants have popped up like so many autumn mushrooms around town. Many are of only average quality, but Shunka is a cut above. The presence of Japanese punters is reassuring, and the open-plan kitchen equally inspires confidence – you can keep an eye on what they're doing with your tempura and sashimi.

☎ 93 412 49 91
✉ Carrer dels Sagristans 5
⏲ lunch & dinner
Tue-Sun Ⓜ Jaume I

Know what'll make this even better? Churros…

EL RAVAL & POBLE SEC

Bar Central (5, C3) $$
Market
Less well known than one of its better published counterparts, this no-nonsense eatery towards the back of Barcelona's emblematic produce market is one of the best of several for a hearty lunch. Marketeers, local workers and the occasional curious tourist jostle for a stool. Go for the grilled fish of the day or perhaps some chunky *mandonguilles* (meatballs).
☎ 93 301 10 98
✉ Mercat de la Boqueria ⏰ lunch Mon-Sat
Ⓜ Liceu ♿ fair

Bar Kasparo (5, C2) $$
Mediterranean
There's atmospheric terrace dining beneath arches at this friendly Australian-run place, which takes over an entire corner of a *plaça* dominated by a relatively calm children's playground. It does a sturdy line in snacks, mixed salads, filled rolls and hot dishes that change daily.
☎ 93 302 20 72
✉ Plaça de Vicenç Martorell 4 ⏰ 10am-10.30pm Ⓜ Catalunya

Biblioteca (5, C4) $$
Mediterranean
In a long ground-floor setting, with bare brick walls and a stylishly simple white décor, the Library presents a changing menu of mixed dishes. The food is rooted in Catalan cooking with the occasional twist, and expands to a more broadly

Panting for Paella?
To save you scanning these pages looking for this Spanish speciality (as well as the various scrumptious Catalan derivatives), try **Set (7) Portes** (p77), **Restaurant Pitarra** (opposite), **Merendero de la Mari** (p81) or **Elche** (p74), all of which are renowned for the rice dish named after the two-handled pan in which it is traditionally served. In many simple eateries, Thursday is traditionally paella day, meaning it comes as a first course in the *menú del día* (set lunch) that day.

Mediterranean range. There's a nice selection of wines, and service is attentive.
☎ 93 412 62 21
✉ Carrer de la Junta del Comerç 28 ⏰ lunch & dinner Tue-Sat Ⓜ Liceu

Biocenter (5, C2) $
Vegetarian
You share your table with whomever at this large and friendly veggie restaurant, serving a great assortment of salads, casseroles and seasonal vegetables cooked using various techniques from around the world. A *combinat* is a good option – you select one of the hot

meals of the day and then heap on salad from the buffet out the back. The owners also run a natural-health-food shop across the road.
☎ 93 301 45 83
✉ Carrer del Pintor Fortuny 25 ⏰ 1-5pm Mon-Sat Ⓜ Liceu Ⓥ

C'al Estevet (5, B1) $$
Catalan
There's nourishment for soul and body at this wonderfully atmospheric old restaurant, where generations of the Suñé family – whose warm and hearty hospitality is unrivalled – have been

enticing customers with their robust brand of Catalan fare for more than a century. You can try anything from a beef fillet to snails from Lleida.
☎ 93 302 41 86 ✉ Carrer de Valldonzella 46 🕑 lunch & dinner Mon-Sat Ⓜ Universitat ♿

Ca L'Isidre (5, A4) $$$
Catalan
Every morning, chefs from this seemingly unremarkable restaurant stuck in a back street away from the madding crowd wander across to the bounteous Mercat de la Boqueria to stock up on the raw materials for the day's cooking. This alone is enough to make one want to treat oneself to a meal here. Grand dining areas sweep back from the entrance, ready to accommodate you for some fine fresh-fish dishes and a frequently changing menu.
☎ 93 441 11 39 ✉ Carrer de les Flors 12 🕑 lunch & dinner Mon-Sat Ⓜ Paral.lel

Casa Leopoldo (5, B3) $$$$
Catalan
Long hidden in the slum alleys of El Raval, this classic has become a helluva lot easier to find since much of the housing was knocked down to make way for La Rambla del Raval and other redevelopment still in the pipeline. Several rambling dining areas, sporting magnificent tiled walls and exposed timber-beam ceilings, make this a fine option. The seafood

Barcelona fosters a rosy view of life

menu is extensive and the wine list strong on local products.
☎ 93 441 30 14 ✉ Carrer de Sant Rafael 24 🕑 lunch & dinner Tue-Sat, lunch Sun Ⓜ Liceu

El Cafetí (5, B3) $$
Catalan
Down a busy arcade, far away from the passing tourist trade, you'll find this faded old-world charmer that feels like a familiar, well-thumbed paperback. Head upstairs to the dining area, cluttered with odds and sods like someone's memories, where you can choose from a mix of rice-based dishes or items like chicken in cream of *cava* (Spanish sparkling wine).
☎ 93 329 24 19 ✉ Passatge de Bernardí, off

Carrer de Sant Rafael 18 🕑 lunch & dinner Tue-Sat, lunch Sun Ⓜ Liceu

Elche (5, A5) $$
Catalan
Some places are just good at what they do, and keep doing it. Hidden away from the busy old-town centre, this old-style restaurant over two floors has been serving up a variety of paellas, rice dishes and *fideuá* since the 1960s. To enliven the atmosphere, order a bottle or two of *turbio*, a simple, cloudy white wine.
☎ 93 441 30 89 ✉ Carrer de Vila i Vilà 71 🕑 lunch & dinner Ⓜ Paral.lel ♿

Elisabets (5, C2) $$
Catalan
Thank God places like this haven't been swept away by

the tide of gleaming, trendy, could-be-anywhere-in-Soho avant-garde locales that are appearing with ever-greater rapidity in this part of town. What about good old solid food that hits the comfort spot? The walls here are lined with old radio sets, and the lunch menu varies daily. Try the *ragú de jabalí* (wild-boar stew).
☎ 93 317 58 26
✉ **Carrer de Elisabets 2-4**
🕑 **lunch Mon-Sat, lunch & dinner Fri**
Ⓜ Catalunya 🚇

Granja Viader (5, C2) $
Dairy Bar
The fifth generation of the same family runs this atmospheric milk bar and café, which was set up in 1873 as the first to bring farm freshness to the city. They invented *cacaolat*, the chocolate-and-skimmed-milk drink now popular all over Spain, and continue to be innovative purveyors of all things milky.
☎ 93 318 34 86 ✉ Carrer d'En Xuclá 4 🕑 9am-

1.45pm & 5-8.45pm Tue-Sat, 5-8.45pm Mon
Ⓜ Liceu 🚇

Organic (5, C4) $
Vegetarian
Like a grand old barn, this vegetarians' paradise-on-earth cooks up a tempting variety of dishes without even a whiff of meat. On the left after you enter is the kitchen, where you place your order. Make your choice from the daily changing menu and then tuck into the salad bar in the middle of the restaurant.
☎ 93 301 09 02
✉ **Carrer de la Junta del Comerç 11** 🕑 1pm-midnight Ⓜ Liceu
🚇 fair 🚇 Ⓥ

Rita Blue (5, C3) $$
Mixed Mediterranean
Run by the same people as Margarita Blue (p71), here the theme is more New York meets the Med. In a sense the formula is similar. Nurse your favourite tipple while waiting to be escorted to a table to the side of and behind the bar. The food is a curious blend of Mexiterranean (*fajitas*, *burritos* et al meets Mallorcan cod). After dinner, head downstairs for a little live music or techno dance until 3am on Friday and Saturday.
☎ 93 412 34 38
✉ **Plaça de St Agustí 3**
🕑 **lunch & dinner Tue-Sat, lunch Sun**
Ⓜ Liceu

Deals & Dinners

Need to impress an incoming client with your local knowledge, and close a deal? Try the following for a classy, authentic Catalan power lunch: **Casa Calvet** (p78), **Ca L'Isidre** (opposite), **Set (7) Portes** (p77), **Hofmann** (p76) or **Agut** (p69).

LA RIBERA

Ábac (8, D3) $$$$
Creative
In business since the turn of the millennium, this minimalist designer den still has the critics raving. Neutral, clean lines and lighting seem deliberately conjured so as not to rob even a sliver of concentration from the imaginative dishes issuing from the kitchen – which might include foie gras steamed in bamboo – that have proven a hit and are

delivered with clockwork precision.
☎ 93 319 66 00
✉ **Carrer del Rec 79-89**
🕑 **lunch & dinner Tue-Sat, dinner Mon**
Ⓜ Barceloneta 🚇 fair

Cal Pep (8, C3) $$$
Tapas
This boisterous tapas bar brims with energy and personality thanks to Pep, the owner and chef, who keeps his customers amused with

a constant stream of banter while he grills the sensational seafood tapas for which this restaurant is famous.
☎ 93 310 79 61
✉ **Plaça de les Olles 8**
🕑 **dinner Mon, lunch & dinner Tue-Sat**
Ⓜ Barceloneta

Centre Cultural Euskal Etxea (8, B2) $$
Basque
One of the more established Basque tapas bars in

Barcelona, this cultural centre still beats many of its flashier newcomer competitors for authenticity and atmosphere. Choose your *pintxos* (snacks), sip *txacoli* wine, and keep the toothpicks so the staff can count them up and work out your bill. You could almost be in San Sebastián.
☎ 93 310 21 85
✉ Placeta de Montcada 1
☽ lunch & dinner Tue-Sat, lunch Sun
Ⓜ Jaume I ♿

Just one more, then…Centre Cultural Euskal Etxea (p75)

Comerç 24 (5, H2) $$
Modern
In the vanguard of Barcelona's modern – dare we say experimental – eateries, this place is a den of variety and extremes. The décor is unremittingly black, the cook an alumnus of Ferran Adriá and the cuisine incredibly eclectic. The emphasis is on waves of bite-sized snacks that traverse the culinary globe with flavours pulled in from all four corners.
☎ 93 319 21 02 ✉ Carrer del Comerç 24 ☽ lunch & dinner Tue-Fri, dinner Sat Ⓜ Arc de Triomf

Comme-Bio (La Botiga) (5, F3) $
Vegetarian
Where vegetarianism is a celebration rather than a chore, large and stylish Comme-Bio has an enormous range of additive- and chemical-free dishes, from creative tapas to sturdy mains. There are vegan meals, organic drinks, English menus on request and a wholefood shop full of handmade products.
☎ 93 319 89 68
✉ Via Laietana 28
☽ lunch & dinner
Ⓜ Jaume I ♿ Ⓥ

El Xampanyet (8, B2) $$
Tapas
As you emerge from the museums on this street you might be snared by the smell of anchovies wafting out of this colourful and charming tapas bar. Its specialities are seafood titbits and *cava*, served in a timeless setting, all colourful tiles and hardwood. The place oozes bonhomie.
☎ 93 319 70 03
✉ Carrer de Montcada 22
☽ lunch & dinner Wed-Sat, lunch Sun Ⓜ Jaume I

Estrella de Plata (5, G4) $$$
Tapas
Top for tapas that you won't find anywhere else, this stylish bar combines elegant table settings, white-clad waiting staff and exquisitely presented 'designer' tapas. Beautiful black-and-white photographs on the walls contrast nicely with the décor and offer an evocative tour of Barcelona's history.
☎ 93 319 60 07
✉ Pla del Palau ☽ lunch & dinner Tue-Sat
Ⓜ Barceloneta

Hofmann (8, A3) $$$$
Mediterranean
Some of the nation's great chefs learned the trade at this cooking-academy-cum-restaurant, and you won't be disappointed with the

---

With a View to…
For magnificent aerial views of Barcelona while you eat, it is impossible to beat the **Torre d'Alta Mar** (p81). For an upstairs view over La Rambla, try **Attic** (p68). Those looking for action all around should grab a stool at **Bar Central** (p73), while some of the best people-watching can be done at an outside table at **Cafè Zurich** (p68).

present students' efforts. An imaginative and constantly changing menu keeps chefs and diners on their toes. Especial care is put into the desserts, and there's a lunch *menú del día* at around €30.
☎ 93 319 58 89
✉ Carrer de l'Argenteria 74 ☽ lunch & dinner Mon-Fri Ⓜ Jaume I

La Flauta Mágica (8, B2) $$
Vegetarian
The menus themselves are a talking point – which album cover is yours on? *Neil Diamond Live? The Cars?* But into the food. A simple burned-orange décor and low lighting set a chilled ambience for a limited menu of veggie dishes (try the *arroz y curry de la sonrisa eterna*, rice and curry of the eternal smile), balanced by a limited selection of dishes for carnivores, all done with free-range products.
☎ 93 268 46 94
✉ Carrer dels Banys Vells 18 ☽ dinner Ⓜ Jaume I Ⓥ

L'Hivernacle (5, H3) $$
Mediterranean
Where else can you sit amid palms and fig trees inside a 19th-century hothouse for dinner and drinks? The relaxed bar is just inside the entrance from Passeig de Picasso. Jazz and classical concerts are often staged here in the evening. The restaurant lies deeper inside the iron-and-glass structure.
☎ 93 295 40 17 ✉ Passeig de Picasso ☽ lunch & dinner Mon-Sat, lunch Sun Ⓜ Arc de Triomf ♿ fair ♿

L'Ou com Balla (8, B2) $$$
Creative French-Moroccan
The candlelit tables and fusion rhythms wafting over the restaurant will have romantic couples nodding their approval. The 'Dancing Egg' presents an eclectic mix of Franco-Moroccan cooking that makes a delicate change from the local fare.
☎ 93 310 53 78 ✉ Carrer dels Banys Vells 20 ☽ dinner Ⓜ Jaume I

Pla de la Garsa (5, G3) $$
Catalan
This staunchly Catalan restaurant was Barcelona's hippest hangout during the twilight of Franco's reign. Scattered with antiques and original 19th-century fixtures, today it's still the most enchanting. The whole Catalan caboodle is good, but the highlights are the superb wines, cheeses and desserts.
☎ 93 315 23 13
✉ Carrer dels Assaonadors 13 ☽ dinner Ⓜ Jaume I

Santa Maria (5, G3) $$$
Tapas
Swing through the doors of this snazzy place for a smorgasbord of gourmet tapas. Beautifully decked out and always busy, its innovative and specialist creations range from falafel to sushi and lots of spins on Spanish favourites (black sausage with anise and orange, anyone?), all prepared with zest.
☎ 93 315 12 27
✉ Carrer del Comerç 17 ☽ lunch & dinner Mon-Sat Ⓜ Jaume I

Set (7) Portes (5, G5) $$$
Catalan
Gilt-framed mirrors and black-and-white-tiled floors reinforce the old-world atmosphere of this Barcelona classic, founded in 1836 and famous for its paella, seafood platters and huge portions. You might sit in a chair previously warmed by the bum of Einstein, Orson Welles, Picasso or Ava Gardner.
☎ 93 319 30 33
✉ Passeig d'Isabel II 14 ☽ lunch & dinner Ⓜ Barceloneta

Coffee Primer & Tea Warning

Coffee comes in three categories and two languages, Catalan and Castilian (Spanish): *cafè amb llet/café con leche* (drunk at breakfast) is coffee with milk, *cafè sol/café solo* is an espresso and a *cafè tallat/café cortado* is an espresso cut with a splash of milk, which you can order hot *(calenta/caliente)* or cold *(freda/fría)*. A *cigaló/carajillo* is an espresso with a shot of alcohol (anything from brandy to Baileys). Barcelonins don't drink much tea, and it's generally black when they do. Request milk separately (*a parte*) and avoid asking for tea in a place where it's not usually served – you'll probably regret it.

L'EIXAMPLE

Alkímia (4, F2) $$$
Creative Catalan
Jordi Vila, an emerging culinary *alquimista*, serves refined Catalan dishes with a twist in this elegant, white-walled restaurant somewhat distant from the tourist trail. The *arròs amb nyora i escarmalans* (rice with crayfish and a sweetish chilli) gives a little kick to the seafood base. Or you could go for a set menu of about a dozen small courses – foodies' heaven.
☎ 93 207 61 15
✉ Carrer de l'Indústria 79 ⏲ lunch & dinner Mon-Fri, dinner Sat
Ⓜ Sagrada Família

Casa Calvet (4, G3) $$$$
Mediterranean
Set on the ground floor of a Gaudí apartment block, this sophisticated restaurant is patronised by VIPs from far and wide, who come here for creative Mediterranean cooking with a Catalan bent. Even if you don't enjoy your foie gras or ravioli stuffed with oysters, you can still savour Gaudí's genius.
☎ 93 412 40 12
✉ Carrer de Casp 48
⏲ lunch & dinner Mon-Sat Ⓜ Urquinaona

Cerveseria Catalana (6, A3) $$
Tapas
You can wander in here for breakfast, lunch and tea. Coffee and croissants are on in the morning, or wait until lunch to enjoy choosing from the cornucopia of tapas and *montaditos*. You can sit at the bar, on the footpath terrace or in the restaurant at the back. The variety of hot tapas, mouth-watering salads and other snacks draws a well-dressed crowd from all over the *barri*.
☎ 93 216 03 68
✉ Carrer de Mallorca 236
⏲ lunch & dinner
Ⓜ Passeig de Gràcia

Ciudad Condal (6, B6) $$
Tapas
Join the smart l'Eixample set and choose from up to 50 different tapas, including salads and *flautas* (tapas served on baguettes). It's cheaper if you eat at the bar, cooler on the terrace and more formal in the restaurant.
☎ 93 318 19 97 ✉ La Rambla de Catalunya 18
⏲ lunch & dinner
Ⓜ Passeig de Gràcia

La Dida (4, F2) $$
Catalan
The big event in this arch-Spanish–looking establishment (lots of timber, dark wrought iron and tiles), one of the few decent eateries near the Sagrada Família, are the weekend rice specials. Dig into a hearty *arròs caldòs* (seafood-and-rice stew). Otherwise, the menu wavers between traditional Catalan and the occasional Med adventure. Seasonal variety is key too, with mushroom specials in October and venison a major theme in November. The place oozes an old-fashioned feel, which will appeal to those yearning to escape the glistening 21st-century modernity of contemporary dining.
☎ 93 207 23 91
✉ Carrer de Roger de Flor 230 ⏲ lunch & dinner Mon-Sat, lunch Sun
Ⓜ Sagrada Família ♿

L'Atzavara (4, E4) $
Vegetarian
Outrageously good value (which is why there are usually queues out the front), this place is nothing special to look at, but the grub is good. The three-course lunch changes daily but always includes salads and international vegetarian favourites such as macaroni and lasagne.
☎ 93 454 59 25
✉ Carrer de Muntaner 109
⏲ lunch Mon-Sat
Ⓜ Hospital Clínic Ⓥ

Mauri (6, A3) $
Café & pastry shop
Join the ladies who lunch for exquisite pastries, light snacks and piped music. The plush interior is capped by an ornately painted fresco at the entrance, which dates back to Mauri's first days in 1929. This is the kind of place that your mum would love…and you will, too, if mouth-watering pastries ring your bell.
☎ 93 215 10 20 ✉ La Rambla de Catalunya 102
⏲ 8am-9pm Mon-Sat, 8am-3pm Sun Ⓜ Diagonal

Semproniana (4, E3) $$
Creative Catalan
At home in a building formerly occupied by a modest publishing house,

the first surprise here is the seemingly chaotic and eclectic décor. Take a seat at the nicely spaced, linen-draped tables and take it all in as you decide on your order. The chef-owner is a member of the Parellada restaurant dynasty, and she cooks up a veritable storm of modern Catalan dishes, which might include *braçet dánec amb poma* (duck leg in a rich sauce, accompanied with diced apple).

☎ 93 453 18 20
✉ **Carrer de Rosselló 148**
🕒 **lunch & dinner Mon-Sat** Ⓜ **Hospital Clínic**

Speakeasy (4, E3) **$$$$**
International
Lurking behind the Dry Martini, a fine cocktail bar, is this classy eatery with a 1930s feel. In the best Prohibition style, you will be shown a door through the kitchen to a 'store-room' lined with hundreds of bottles of quality tipples, where your table awaits. The clientele are often business chaps and dames in furs. The menu depends partly on the markets, but the carpaccio Dry Martini, a heavenly light meat treat, is one of the signature dishes.

☎ 93 217 50 80
✉ **Carrer d'Aribau 162-166** 🕒 **lunch & dinner Mon-Fri, dinner Sat** Ⓜ **Diagonal**

Taktika Berri (4, E4) **$$$**
Basque & tapas
Deep in the grid maze of L'Eixample is this Basque redoubt. You have two choices: hang around the

Winning Ways of Catalan Wines

Catalan wine (*vi/vino*) is an adventure all on its own. Some fine drops are produced across the region, some by international names and others by small farms. The Penedès region, about 40km southwest of Barcelona, is the biggest producer, more than doubling the production in the rest of Catalonia. It is best known for its *cava* (Spanish sparkling wine; Freixenet and Codorníu are name brands around the world), and a host of whites (*blanc/blanco*). Red (*negre/tinto*) and rosé (*rosat/rosado*) are produced in smaller quantities. Torres is the biggest name in Catalan still wines, but it's worth trying smaller operators such as Nadal and Mas Tinell. Other outstanding wine-region labels to look for are Priorat (strong, quality reds) and Raïmat (reds and whites).

bar (just try at the lunch rush hour!) and nibble away at the army of Basque-style tapas – the trick is to grab them from the waitress as she transports them from the kitchen to the bar – or head out the back for a slap-up sit-down meal.

☎ 93 453 47 59
✉ **Carrer de València 169**
🕒 **lunch & dinner Mon-Fri, lunch Sat**
Ⓜ **Hospital Clinic**

Tragaluz (6, B3) **$$$**
Mediterranean
This restaurant is named after the spectacular sky-light that crowns the dining room. The food is fab, drawing inspiration from all over the Mediterranean (don't skip dessert), and there's an equally cool cocktail lounge downstairs.

☎ 93 487 01 96
✉ **Passatge de la Concepció 5** 🕒 **lunch & dinner** Ⓜ **Diagonal**

GRÀCIA

Botafumeiro (7, A2) $$$$
Galician/Seafood
The seafood in this Galician treasure is about as fresh as you'll get without getting wet. Lobster, scallops, oysters and shellfish are kept in a Jacuzzi, waiting to be served at business dinners and family occasions in the bustling restaurant. Guitar players and singers contribute to the cheerful clamour.
☎ 93 218 42 30 ✉ Carrer Gran de Gràcia 81 ⏱ 1pm-1am Ⓜ Fontana

Flash Flash (4, E3) $
Spanish
Barcelona's first-ever designer bar is the height of 1970s cool, with long, luxurious leather banquettes and white walls adorned with pictures of a Twiggy-esque photographer prancing about taking snaps. The menu consists of hundreds of different omelettes (*tortillas*), including some for dessert. In spite of its years, it remains as popular as ever for a bright

and varied in-crowd up in this posh end of town.
☎ 93 237 09 90 ✉ Carrer de Granada del Penedès 25 ⏱ 1pm-1am 🚉 FCG Gràcia Ⓥ

Jean-Luc Figueras (6, B1) $$$$
Catalan/French
One of the jewels in the crown of Barcelona's food scene, everything about this restaurant – right down to the crayon-drawn individual menus – has the mark of head chef and renowned local foodie Jean-Luc Figueras. The food, Catalan with French flair, is exceptional and the décor elegantly understated. Service is a little rushed.
☎ 93 415 28 77 ✉ Carrer de Santa Teresa 10 ⏱ lunch & dinner Mon-Sat Ⓜ Diagonal

La Singular (7, C3) $$
Mediterranean
The menu at this cosy restaurant depends on what

caught the chef's eye at the market that day. It's obvious that the creative cooks get as much of a kick out of seasonal produce as the folks of Gràcia who make bookings near-essential here. At lunch only a set menu is on offer, and salads are the forte.
☎ 93 237 50 98 ✉ Carrer de Francisco Giner 50 ⏱ lunch Mon-Thu, lunch & dinner Fri & Sat Ⓜ Diagonal Ⓥ

Sol Soler (7, B2) $$
Tapas
On a corner of Gràcia's most lively *plaça*, this busy wholefood tapas bar has faded bohemian chic, relaxed music, intimate lighting and marble tables on which to enjoy a range of tasty and, in part, vegetarian fare.
☎ 93 217 44 40 ✉ Plaça del Sol 21-22 ⏱ 5pm-1.30am Mon, 3pm-2am Tue-Fri, 1pm-2.30am Sat, 1pm-2am Sun Ⓜ Fontana Ⓥ

Specchio Magico (7, B3) $$$
Italian
Calm and charming, this tiny Italian joint is perfect for intimate get-togethers and is one of the most reliable Italian options in town. Among the usual fare, you can enjoy wonderfully soothing vegetable and chicken terrines in summer, and the desserts are simply *fantastici*.
☎ 93 415 33 71 ✉ Carrer de Luis Antúnez 3 ⏱ lunch & dinner Ⓜ Diagonal

Market Cuisine
Many of the restaurants listed here specialise in 'market cuisine', which means that their constantly changing menus are based on whatever looks best at the market each morning rather than a particular style of cooking or category of cuisine.

LA BARCELONETA

Agua (4, J4) $$$
Mediterranean
One of several hip locales to have opened for your mandibles' pleasure along the Barceloneta beachfront in the past few years, Agua offers a brightly lit and spacious inside dining area at beach level, as well as an alfresco option for those balmy summer evenings. Food is bright, with a mix of Spanish, Italian and international influences to keep you on your toes.
☎ 93 225 12 72
✉ **Passeig Marítim de la Barceloneta 30** ☽ **lunch & dinner** Ⓜ **Ciutadella Vila Olímpica** ♿ **fair**

Can Solé (4, H5) $$$
Seafood
For a memorable meal, head to this century-old seafood restaurant where the selection is *staggering*, the food outstanding and the service little short of amazing – when you're halfway through your fish, waiters saunter over, remove it, and discreetly strip away all the bones for you.
☎ 93 221 50 12
✉ **Carrer de Sant Carles 4, La Barceloneta** ☽ **lunch & dinner Tue-Sat, lunch Sun** Ⓜ **Barceloneta**

Merendero de la Mari (5, G6) $$$
Seafood
On a bright sunny day there is little more enticing than donning your shades and basking at a portside terrace table here for an aroma-filled seafood luncheon feast. It does classics (various paellas, *fideuá*) and a range of fish, steamed or grilled. Add a crisp Penedès white and you'll find it hard to get up again to resume sightseeing!
☎ 93 221 31 41 ✉ **Plaça de Pau Vila 1** ☽ **lunch & dinner** Ⓜ **Barceloneta** ♿ **good** 🚼

Torre d'Alta Mar (4, H5) $$$$
Mediterranean
Lately the views on the food here have been a little mixed. But no-one can gainsay the extraordinary views from this tower high above the Barcelona skyline. The kitchen produces a wide range of mostly Mediterranean offerings, and some fine local wines lurk in the cellars. A romantic winner for location alone.
☎ 93 221 00 07
✉ **Torre de Sant Sebastiá, Passeig de Joan de Borbó 88** ☽ **lunch & dinner Tue-Sat, lunch Mon** 🚌 **Nos 17, 39 & 64** ♿ **fair**

Vaso de Oro (5, G6) $$
Tapas
If you like noisy, crowded bars, high-speed bar staff always ready with a smile and a wisecrack, a cornucopia of tapas and a sense that things haven't much changed, come to the 'Glass of Gold' on the edge of La Barceloneta.
☎ 93 319 30 98
✉ **Carrer de Balboa 6** ☽ **11am-midnight** Ⓜ **Barceloneta**

Go on, then, let's have another bottle of wine…

Entertainment

Barcelona knows how to party, especially Thursday to Saturday nights. The lower end of the Barri Gòtic, the hip El Born area and parts of El Raval are all busy, with bars of all descriptions. In L'Eixample, the main axis is along Carrer d'Aribau and up into the chichi area around Carrer de Tuset and Carrer de Marià Cubí. The squares and some streets of Gràcia also hop. Clubs are spread out across these areas and beyond. The heart of gay Barcelona is the 'Gaixample', a cluster of bars, clubs and saunas around Carrer del Consell de Cent west of Passeig de Gràcia.

If symphonies and string quartets are more your thing, choose between venerable music halls and hi-tech auditoriums. The city is a hotbed of contemporary dance, and if that's too energetic for you, a host of cinemas offers everything from vanguard art house to Hollywood schlock. The calendar is crammed with holidays, festivals and headline concerts.

The green fairy at Bar Marsella (p84)

To experience the city in its natural light, you'll have to adjust to going out (much) later. Barcelonins are still in front of the mirror by the time you're usually in full flight; bars are empty until 10pm and clubbers don't even tap their feet before 2am.

The *Guía del Ocio* (€1) is a reasonable general-listings weekly in Castilian. Other magazines, partly or wholly in English, that provide an overall view of what's happening include *BCN Inside* and *Movin' BCN*. Similar is the Spanish *Salir Salir Barcelona*. Keep an eye on the Friday *Què Fem* supplement (in Catalan) in *La Vanguardia* newspaper, and for bars search out free magazines like *Micro, Go Mag* and *Salir,* distributed in many bars in the Ciutat Vella. For information on classical events, get the monthly *Informatiu Musical* leaflet, which is available through tourist offices. *El País* newspaper has a good daily section on cinema and theatre.

Picking up Tickets

You can get hold of *entradas* (tickets) for most venues through the Caixa de Catalunya's **Tel-Entrada service** (☎ 902 101212; www.telentrada.com) or **ServiCaixa** (☎ 902 332211; www.servicaixa.com). At some of the latter's ATMs you can also purchase tickets. There's a *venta de localidades* (ticket office) on the ground floor of the **El Corte Inglés** (☎ 902 400222; http://entradas.elcorteingles.es) on Plaça de Catalunya and at the FNAC store (p61) on the same square.

You can buy same-day half-price tickets to some events at the Caixa de Catalunya desk in the tourist office on Plaça de Catalunya (p34).

Special Events

January *New Year's Eve* – people eat a grape for each chime, for luck
Cavalcada dels Reis – on the 5th, three kings arrive by sea and parade through the city, launching thousands of sweeties at delighted kiddies
Festes dels Tres Tombs – week-long festival in the district of Sant Antoni, beginning on the 17th

February *Carnestoltes* – parade and parties late in the month to open *carnaval* (carnival); coincides with *Festes de Santa Eulàlia*, the celebration of one of Barcelona's two patron saints with concerts and cultural events

March–April *Divendres Sant (Good Friday)* – southern Spanish–style three-hour procession with religious floats, sombre drumming and music; it proceeds from the Església de Sant Agustí in El Raval to the Catedral

April *Dia de Sant Jordi* – the 23rd is the day of Catalonia's patron saint and the Day of the Book; men give women roses, women give men books
Feria de Abril – late in the month there are 10 days of Andalucían flamenco, food and carousing

May *Sant Ponç* – on the 11th there's a quaint market in Carrer de l'Hospital commemorating the patron saint of beekeepers and herbalists

June *L'Ou com Balla* – 'dancing eggs' celebrates Corpus Christi some time in the first half of the month
Sonar – a superb three-day music festival of electronica and multimedia
Dia per l'Alliberament Lesbià i Gai – gay and lesbian festival and parade
Festa de la Música – free music concerts in the streets on the 21st
Festival del Grec – city-wide performing-arts festival into August
Nit del Foc – fireworks, bonfires and merrymaking for the 'night of fire' on the 23rd, prior to the Dia de Sant Joan (feast of St John) on the 24th

August *Festa Major de Gràcia* – Gràcia's massive, week-long festival mid-month; lively street decorations, food stands, concerts in the squares and general sleeplessness
Festa Major de Sants – the festival of Sants, late in the month

September *Diada* – it's Catalan national day on the 11th; flag-waving and speeches
Festes de la Mercè – the 24th is the big one: four days of festivities, with a packed music concert programme, *castellers* (human-castle builders), folk dancing, parades of *gegants* (giants) and *capgrossos* (big heads), and a huge *correfoc* (fire race)
Festa Major de la Barceloneta – dancing and drinking in La Barceloneta
Mostra de Vins i Caves de Catalunya – four-day food-and-wine festival in Port Vell, beginning on the 24th

November *Festival International de Jazz de Barcelona* – jazz around the city

December *Fira de Santa Llúcia* – Christmas market by the Catedral from the first to the 24th

BARS & PUBS

Bar Marsella (5, B4) This place has been in the same family for five generations and looks like it hasn't had a lick of paint since it was first opened in 1820. Assorted chandeliers, tiles and mirrors decorate its one big room, which on weekends is packed to its rickety rafters with a cheerful mishmash of shady characters, drag queens and slumming uptowners, who stop by to try the absinthe. Signs from the Franco era prohibiting singing still adorn the walls.
☎ 93 442 72 63
✉ **Carrer de Sant Pau 65, El Raval** 🕙 **10pm-2am Mon-Thu, 10pm-3am Fri & Sat** Ⓜ **Liceu**

Bar Pastís (5, C5) No bigger than a postage stamp, this bar was opened after WWII by a Catalan couple infatuated with Marseilles. They dedicated it to French cabaret, and had only Edith Piaf on the stereo and a drinks list comprising *pastis*. There are more drinks on offer these days, but the character remains the same.
☎ 93 318 79 80 ✉ **Carrer de Santa Mònica 4, El Raval** 🕙 **7.30pm-3am Tue-Sun** Ⓜ **Drassanes**

Barcelona Pipa Club (5, D4) Ring the buzzer at one of the most intriguing bars in the city. It's a genuine pipe-smokers' club by day and is transformed into a dim, laid-back and incurably cool bar at night. King Juan Carlos could walk in and drop his pants and nobody would bat an eyelid.
☎ 93 302 47 32
✉ **Plaça Reial 3, Barri Gòtic** 🕙 **11pm-3am Mon-Sat** Ⓜ **Liceu**

Boadas (5, C2) The founder of this 1933 Art Deco cocktail bar learned his craft serving Hemingway in the famed Floridita bar in Havana, so you know you're in for a class act. The walls are covered with mementos, including a sketch by Miró of the contented customers who've got themselves sloshed on the hundreds of enticing cocktails on offer here.
☎ 93 318 95 92
✉ **Carrer dels Tallers 1, El Raval** 🕙 **noon-2am Mon-Thu, noon-3am Fri & Sat** Ⓜ **Catalunya**

Bocayma (4, D3) One of the best meeting places in this chichi uptown bar zone, Bocayma starts in fairly quiet fashion with people gathered around its little tables. After midnight the music begins to rev up and punters become animated, readying for a outing to nearby clubs. It's not uncommon to find this spot open beyond its official hours.
✉ **Carrer de l'Avenir 50, Sant Gervasi** 🕙 **11pm-2am Tue-Wed, 11pm-3am Thu-Sat** 🚇 **FGC Muntaner**

Buda Barcelona (4, G3) The name bar and restaurant that is all the rage in

They do Papa Hemingway proud at Boadas

Chillin' on the Beach

Summer lounging on the beaches of Barcelona is not just about towels on the sand. Scattered along the beaches running northeast from Port Olímpic is a series of hip little beach bars bringing the best in chilled club sounds to the seaside. Generally, they are all similar: set in timber platforms, surrounded by greenery and in some cases serving a little food. The atmosphere can change radically from one to another – wander along and find one that suits. Sip on your favourite cocktail as you take in the last rays of the day. And there's no need to head straight home at sundown, as these places keep humming until 1am. All those beautifully tanned bodies hanging on the beach – day and night!

Nearest Port Olímpic on Platja de la Nova Icària is **Dockers** (4, J3), while three similar spots are spread along the next beach, Platja de Bogatell. One of the more popular places is **Mochima** (www.mochimabar.com) on the following beach, Platja de Mar Bella.

Paris (how many CDs is it going to put out?) has its equally chic branch in the heart of L'Eixample. Come to eat, or pop in later for drinks at this luxurious Oriental den, and chill amid the beaming Buddhas. If you opt for nosh, you're in for a mix of Indian, Japanese and Mediterranean munching.

☎ 93 318 42 52
✉ Carrer de Pau Claris 92, L'Eixample € free
🕐 9pm-3am
Ⓜ Urquinaona

Café Que Pone Muebles Navarro (5, B3) This laid-back bar-cum-lounge-cum-art-space is the perfect spot for a quiet one or two and some long rambling chats while comfortably sunk into a sofa or gathered round a small back-of-the-truck table. Any more chilled than this place and you'd be in deep freeze.
✉ Carrer de la Riera Alta 4-6, El Raval
🕐 6pm-midnight Tue-Thu & Sun, 6pm-2am Fri & Sat Ⓜ Sant Antoni

Café Royale (5, D4)
These are some of the most sought after sofas in Barcelona, perfect for chilling out with warm lighting, a good-looking crowd, and irresistible soul, funk and bossa fusions. It gets terribly packed with visitors at the weekend. That's no surprise, as it's one of the grooviest early-evening dance options in town.
☎ 93 317 61 24
✉ Carrer Nou de Zurbano 3, Barri Gòtic
🕐 6pm-2.30am
Ⓜ Liceu

Casa Almirall (5, B2)
People have been boozing here since 1860, which makes it the oldest continuously functioning bar in Barcelona. Delightfully dishevelled, it still has its original Modernista bar, much loved by punters and loathed (for its cramped-ness) by staff.
✉ Carrer de Joaquín Costa 33, El Raval
🕐 7pm-2.30am Sun-Thu, 7pm-3am Fri & Sat Ⓜ Universitat

CDLC (4, J4)
The Carpe Diem Lounge Club is one of the hippest locales on Barcelona's waterfront. A mix of pseudo-Oriental (à la Buda Barcelona) and Med, with a partly outdoor lounge area, chilled music, occasional live performances and beautiful customers, makes this place irresistible to the abfab crowd.
☎ 93 224 04 70
✉ Passeig Marítim de la Barceloneta 32, La Barceloneta 🕐 noon-3am
Ⓜ Ciutadella Vila Olímpica

Daguiri (4, H5) This grungy seaside bar was made for its young, travelling crowd – the kind who have elected to hang out in Barcelona for a stretch and prefer to avoid the crush of the old town centre. You can have a light meal or just sip a summertime beer inside or outside.
☎ 93 221 51 09
✉ Carrer de Grau i Torras 59, La Barceloneta
🕐 10am-midnight
Ⓜ Barceloneta

Solo Visitors

Drinking alone needn't be an unpleasant experience in Barcelona's bars. Anything can happen really, so take courage and head out into the night! Some of the late-night bars in the old town, such as **London Bar** (below), fill up with all sorts of people, local and foreign, opening up possibilities for contact. As in any city, clubs are always potentially interesting for singles on the lookout. **Sutton Club** (p88) is a classy choice full of singles but not sleaze.

Dot Light Club (5, D5)

This little treasure, in the backstreets of atmospheric Barri Gòtic, glows with different theme nights throughout the week. There's a cosy red-lit bar at the front for a chat or a snuggle, and a small, congenial dance floor out the back, which is creatively illuminated with projections of cult movies.
☎ 93 302 70 26
🖵 www.dotlightclub .com ✉ Carrer Nou de Sant Francesc, Barri Gòtic € free 🕒 10pm-2.30am Sun & Tue-Thu, 10pm-3am Fri & Sat Ⓜ Drassanes

La Tinaja (8, C3)

The enormous, centuries-old vaulted space of this one-time warehouse is decorated with huge old *tinajas* (amphorae) and is a perfectly congenial location to tipple happily on local wines, which can be accompanied earlier in the evening by ham, cheese and pâté platters or even a full meal if you like.
☎ 93 310 22 50
✉ Carrer de l'Espertería 9, La Ribera 🕒 5pm-2am Ⓜ Barceloneta

La Vinya del Senyor (8, B3)

A wine-taster's fantasy, this bar has a stunning location looking out over the Santa Maria del Mar church. You can choose from almost 300 varieties of wine and *cava* (Spanish sparkling wine) from around the world, and enjoy inventive *platillos* (mini-tapas) as you sip your drink. The table by the window upstairs provides one of the best views in the city.
☎ 93 310 33 79
✉ Plaça de Santa Maria del Mar 5, La Ribera 🕒 noon-1am Tue-Sun Ⓜ Jaume I

Les Gens Que J'Aime (6, C4)

Incurably romantic, this basement bar in l'Eixample combines candlelight and privacy with antique red-velvet sofas and dark wood furniture and trims. It's the perfect place for a night of sweet nothings.
☎ 93 215 68 79 ✉ Carrer de València 286, L'Eixample 🕒 6pm-2.30am Ⓜ Passeig de Gràcia

London Bar (5, C4)

In the heart of the once notorious Barri Xinés district, this bar was founded in 1910 as a hangout for circus hands, and drew the likes of Picasso and Miró in search of local colour. With the occasional band playing out the back and a wonderful mix of local customers and travellers, it remains a classic.
☎ 93 318 52 61 ✉ Carrer Nou de la Rambla 34, El Raval 🕒 7pm-5am Tue-Sun Ⓜ Drassanes

Mirablau (4, C1)

For the most stunning views of Barcelona – and the spectacle of the city's rich and famous dancing badly – catch a cab to this chichi bar and club perched on top of Tibidabo. Doormen come on for the club at 11pm, and it helps if you're wearing coloured corduroys or Prada if you want to get past them.
☎ 93 418 58 79 ✉ Plaça del Doctor Andreu, Tibidabo 🕒 bar 11am-5am Sun-Thu, 11am-6am Fri-Sat 🚉 FGC Tibidabo, then Tramvia Blau or take a taxi

Palau Dalmases – Espai Barroc (8, B2)

Perhaps the most pretentious bar in town, this 'baroque space' occupies a handsome 14th-century palace and is awash with period splendour (or naff bric-a-brac, depending on your mood). Drinks are limited to wine and punch, and prices are futuristic, but the place is unique – and unmissable.
☎ 93 310 06 73
✉ Carrer de Montcada 20, La Ribera 🕒 8pm-2am Tue-Sat, 6-10pm Sun Ⓜ Jaume I

Va de Vi waits expectantly for its date

Pitín (8, D2) Several decades before the El Born district became the hippest happening in old-town Barcelona, this stylish, cramped and welcoming bar was pouring out liquid consolation to all and sundry. Up the spiralling staircase is the perfect spot to launch yourself into a big night.
☎ 93 319 50 87
✉ Passeig del Born 34, La Ribera
🕑 6pm-2am Mon-Fri, noon-3am Sat & Sun
Ⓜ Jaume I

Va de Vi (8, B2) This beautifully sedate wine bar has been carved out beneath the lofty arches of a huge 15th-century Gothic structure. Enjoy a respectable selection of local wines by the *copa* (glass) or bottle, and accompany with nibbles and chatter.
☎ 93 319 29 00
✉ Carrer dels Banys Vells 16, La Ribera
🕑 6pm-2am Ⓜ Jaume I

Party Port

If bumping and grinding against sweaty torsos and scantily clad dancers is your thing, head down to Port Olímpic (4, J4) after midnight on weekends, where stacks of indistinguishable clubs provide pumping Spanish chart hits to testosterone-laden men and outnumbered women determined to party.

DANCE CLUBS

See also the Rock, Jazz & Blues section (p90) as several places that stage live music double as clubs.

Moog (5, C5) Moog (named after the synthesiser) is reliable for techno and electronica, and is always packed with a young, enthusiastic crowd. Bigger in stature than in size, it attracts lots of big-name DJs. Upstairs specialises in retro Latin dance.
☎ 93 301 72 82
🖥 www.masimas.com
✉ Carrer de l'Arc del Teatre 3, El Raval € €8
🕑 11.30pm-5am
Ⓜ Drassanes

Otto Zutz (4, E2) This converted three-storey warehouse used to be the hippest club in Barcelona, patronised by international stars of every ilk. Inevitably, the wannabes and expensive dressers have replaced the celebrities, but the gritty elegance remains, and this is still a great place to dance. There's a different vibe on the three floors (top floor is VIPs only), linked by a giant atrium.
☎ 93 238 07 22
✉ Carrer de Lincoln 15, Sant Gervasi € €15
🕑 midnight-5.30am Tue-Sat 🚊 FGC Gràcia

Sutton Club (4, E3)
An uptown honey pot, this place doesn't get happening until all the surrounding bars start closing their doors. It's a den of beautiful people, but the central dance area (complete with go-go girls and boys), surrounded arena-style by seating and several strategically placed bars, will draw you in. One reason for arriving a little before the crowds (from 2am) is that it increases your chances of getting past the bouncers.
☎ 93 414 42 17
✉ Carrer de Tuset 13,

La Paloma
The 100-year-old **La Paloma** (5, A1; ☎ 93 301 68 97; Carrer del Tigre 27; ⊗ 11pm-5am Thu-Sat; metro Universitat) is a unique local institution and an essential night out in Barcelona. The evening starts with the band playing cha-chas and tangos to a chirpy crowd of mostly middle-aged couples. At 1am it transforms into the Bongo Lounge, when DJs take over and the beautiful young things stream in. The music gets harder as the night wears on. Catch the last half-hour of the band (avoiding the queues) and nab a table along the balcony to admire the faded grandeur of the room.

L'Eixample € €12
⊗ 11.30pm-6am Tue-Sat
Ⓜ Diagonal

Terrrazza (1, A1) Move to 'the terrace' for rejuvenation when you run out of steam. Some of the biggest international names play at this summertime must, which can be relied on for some of the meatiest dance tunes on vinyl and for a clientele comprising extremely high-quality eye candy. In winter the club moves indoors and becomes Discothèque.
☎ 93 423 12 85 🖳 www.nightsungroup.com
✉ Avinguda del Marquès de Comillas (Poble Espanyol) € €18 ⊗ midnight-7am Fri & Sat Ⓜ Espanya

Mellow out at one of Barcelona's many fine bars

CINEMAS

Films shown in their original languages with subtitles are identified in listings by the letters VO *(versió original)*. The best movie listings are in the daily *El País* newspaper. Getting a ticket at the door (generally €5.50 to €6) will only be a problem on weekend evenings, and in most cinemas you can get advance tickets. Monday or Wednesday is discount night in many cinemas (€4 to €4.50). In addition to the following mainstream and art-house cinemas, classic movies are sometimes shown in such diverse locations as La Pedrera (p16), Apolo (p90), FNAC record and book store in the El Triangle shopping centre on Plaça de Catalunya (p34), CaixaForum (p27) and the Centre de Cultura Contemporània de Barcelona (CCCB; p27).

Casablanca (6, B1) The non-mainstream and art-house releases shown on these screens are generally worth a look. The only problem is that the seats are perversely uncomfortable and no amount of popcorn can take your mind off it.
☎ 93 218 43 45
✉ Passeig de Gràcia 115, L'Eixample ☷ 4 sessions, the last around 10.15pm
€ €5.50 Ⓜ Diagonal

Filmoteca (4, D3) This government-funded gem specialises in programmes that group films together by particular directors, styles, eras and countries. Some films may be decades old, while others are still in the cinemas. The programmes change daily – pick up the fortnightly schedules directly from the cinema.
☎ 93 410 75 90
✉ Avda de Sarrià 31-33, Sarrià ☷ 5.30pm (sometimes a children's show), 7.30pm & 10pm € €2.70 Ⓜ Hospital Clínic

Icària Yelmo Cineplex (4, J3) Behind the Port Olímpic, this is a typical multiplex, with 15 screens predominantly screening exclusively VO movies, both mainstream and art house. The place is pretty dispiriting in itself but presents the single greatest concentration of movies in their original language in Barcelona.
☎ 93 221 75 85
🖳 www.yelmocineplex.es, in Castilian ✉ Carrer de Salvador Espriu 61, Vila

Olímpica € €6 ☷ up to 6 sessions 11am-10.30pm, plus movie after midnight Fri & Sat Ⓜ Ciutadella Vila Olímpica

Imax (5, F6) When there's a decent flick made for this screen format – apart from nature documentaries – this will be a great place to see it. It offers a choice of formats including Omnimax and three-D. Most of the documentaries are VO.
☎ 93 225 11 11
✉ Moll d'Espanya, Port Vell € €8 ☷ 10.15am-10.30pm Mon-Sun Ⓜ Barceloneta

Méliès Cinemes (4, E4) This two-screen movie house specialises in showing original versions of old classics, and fills the gap between the sometimes dry intellectualism of the Filmoteca and the Hollywood excesses of the multiplexes.
☎ 93 451 00 51
✉ Carrer de Villarroel

102, L'Eixample € €4.50 ☷ 4 sessions 5-10.15pm Ⓜ Urgell

Verdi (7, C2) This cinematic institution is highly regarded for championing creations left of centre and was the first to specialise in VO. Long queues are frequent, especially at weekends.
☎ 93 238 79 90
✉ Carrer de Verdi 32, Gràcia € €5.50 ☷ 4 sessions 4.30-10.45pm, plus movie after midnight Fri & Sat Ⓜ Fontana

Verdi Park (7, C2) The second cinema in the Verdi family. This expansion to the next street means that you have a total of nine VO screens to choose from in Gràcia.
☎ 93 238 79 90
✉ Carrer de Torrijos 49, Gràcia € €5.50
☷ 4 sessions 4.30-10.45pm, plus movie after midnight Fri & Sat Ⓜ Fontana

---

With a Friend Like Sergi...

With an easy charm bred into him on the sunny Catalan coast, Sergi López (1965–) has made a splash in the European cinema world. Starring as the bad guy in Stephen Frears' *Dirty Pretty Things* in 2003, about the nasty side of illegal-migrant life in London, the affable genius of the screen had long ago stolen the hearts of filmgoers on both sides of the Pyrenees. Born in Vilanova i la Geltrú, just southwest of Barcelona, he has starred in the hit French comedy-thriller *Harry, Un Ami Qui Vous Veut Du Bien* (With a Friend Like Harry, 2000) and Spanish flicks such as *Entre las Piernas* (Between Your Legs, 1999) with Spanish stars Victoria Abril and Javier Bardem.

ROCK, JAZZ & BLUES

Apolo (5, A5) It's well worth checking out what's on at this busy and atmospheric old music hall. An eclectic programme of gigs ranges from world music to touring rock bands that you'll never again see in a venue so cosy. Gigs frequently start earlier than the general opening times listed. After the encores, shirty security staff clear the hall for the 'Nitsaclub' dance bash.
☎ 93 301 00 90
🖳 www.nitsa.com, in Castilian ✉ Carrer

Nou de la Rambla 113, Poble Sec € €6-9
🕑 12.30am-5am Wed-Sat, 10.30pm-3.30am Sun
Ⓜ Paral.lel

Bikini (4, D3) The reincarnation of a legendary club that was torn down in 1990 to make way for a shopping mall, the modern Bikini is regarded by many as the best venue in Barcelona, with crisp acoustics and diverse programming.
☎ 93 322 08 00
🖳 www.bikinibcn.com
✉ Carrer Déu i Mata 105,

Les Corts € €10-20
🕑 midnight-5am Tue-Sat
Ⓜ Entença

Harlem Jazz Club (5, E4) Deep in the Barri Gòtic, this is a stalwart of the local scene and the first stop for jazz aficionados. Sessions include traditional and contemporary jazz along with creative fusions from around the world. The scarcity of tables contributes to the club's relaxed and friendly atmosphere.
☎ 93 310 07 55
✉ Carrer de la Comtessa

Sardana – The Catalan Folk Dance

Catalans take their national dance, the *sardana*, seriously (it is not a dance accompanied by peals of laughter). A lot of holding hands and bobbing up and down, and the occasional two-step to the left and back again, it is about as exciting to watch as the proverbial paint drying, but as an affirmation of Catalan identity it has its own particular charm. The music, by turns melancholic and jolly, is played by a reed-and-brass band called a *cobla*, and most of it was written by the 19th century. The origins of the dance are unclear, but the first written reference was in the 16th century. Popular assurances that the *sardana* was banned under Franco are hotly disputed by those who have taken the trouble to study the period.

Sardanas are danced at traditional festivals, but the most likely chance you'll have of seeing them is in front of the **Catedral** (p15; 7pm Wed, 6.30-8.30pm Sat, noon-2pm Sun).

de Sobradiel 8, Barri Gòtic (€) up to €10 ⏰ 8pm-4am Tue-Thu & Sun, 8pm-5am Fri & Sat Ⓜ Jaume I

Jamboree (5, D4) Better as a pulsating gig venue than the club it turns into afterwards, this wildly popular cellar hosts local and international names in everything from jazz to hip-hop. The club – cranking R & B and soul downstairs, and Latin fusion up top – attracts some dodgy-looking characters at the weekend. ☎ 93 319 17 89 🖳 www.masimas.com ✉ Plaça Reial 17, Barri Gòtic (€) up to €10 ⏰ 10.30pm-5am Ⓜ Liceu

Jazz Sí Club (5, A2)
If you want to see who'll be playing at the other venues next time you visit, head to this delightfully disordered club-café run by a contemporary music school. It's a meeting place for musos, with diverse live music early every night. ☎ 93 329 00 20 ✉ Carrer de Requesens 2, El Raval

She's no dodgy-looking character…must be a weekday

(€) from €2 ⏰ 9-11pm Ⓜ Sant Antoni

La Boîte (4, D3) A local institution and a must for jazz, soul and blues fans, this highly regarded uptown basement was the first music venue of the entrepreneurial Mas brothers, doyens of the local entertainment scene. ☎ 93 319 17 89 🖳 www.masimas.com ✉ Avinguda Diagonal 477, L'Eixample (€) €3-15 ⏰ 11pm-5.30am Tue-Sat 🚌 6, 7, 33, 34, 63, 67 & 68

Luz de Gas (4, E3) Anything goes at this large and happening music hall that hosts residencies and big international names from the worlds of soul, country, salsa, rock, jazz, pop and cabaret in a beautiful *belle époque* setting. The versatile place converts into a thumping club later in the night. ☎ 93 209 77 11 ✉ Carrer de Muntaner 246, L'Eixample (€) up to €20 ⏰ gigs from 10pm, club midnight-5am Ⓜ Diagonal

FLAMENCO

Sala Tarantos (5, D4)
Upstairs from the Jamboree (see above) you'll find locals and tourists getting hot and steamy with flamenco, Latin and salsa sessions. As well as the long-established flamenco *tablao* (show), which starts around 10.15pm, you can catch the occasional concert with big-name

acts. Afterwards, the theme carries on with the club's irresistible Latin mix, and you can wander over into Jamboree (with which it is connected). ☎ 93 318 30 67, flamenco show 616 80 34 97 ✉ Plaça Reial 17, Barri Gòtic (€) from €3 ⏰ 10pm-5am Mon-Sat Ⓜ Liceu

Soniquete (5, E5) Pop along for the occasional impromptu flamenco sessions in this tile-lined, friendly bar. When there's no live music the atmosphere retains a flamenco feel, with hot-blooded tunes and a suitably smoky, relaxed atmosphere. ✉ Carrer de Milans 5, Barri Gòtic (€) free ⏰ 9pm-3am Thu-Sun Ⓜ Jaume I

The proud grace of flamenco

Tablao de Carmen (1, A1)
Named after the great Barcelonin *bailaora* (flamenco dancer) Carmen Amaya, this place features a very swanky and lively flamenco show with a full complement of guitarists, singers and dancers. It's not as touristy as you might expect, dinner is decent, and you can save yourself the entrance fee to Poble Espanyol if you book in advance. ☎ 93 325 68 95 🖳 www.tablaodecarmen.com ✉ Carrer dels Arcs 9, Poble Espanyol € show only €29, dinner & show €55 ⏱ shows 9.30pm & 11.30pm Tue-Sun Ⓜ Espanya

CLASSICAL MUSIC, OPERA, DANCE & THEATRE

Barcelona is home to a host of theatres and stages for everything from opera to modern dance. Ticket prices in all cases vary greatly and depend largely on the performance.

Gran Teatre del Liceu (5, C4) Promoted as one of the most technologically advanced theatres in the world, the reconstructed opera house (the original was destroyed by fire in 1994) is a fabulously plush setting for your favourite aria. World-class dance companies also strut their stuff across its esteemed stage, which also sometimes plays host to classical-music concerts. Ticket prices depend on the seats' proximity to the stage, with the cheapest affording no view of it. ☎ 93 485 99 13 🖳 www.liceubarcelona.com ✉ La Rambla dels Caputxins 51-59 € €7.50-150 ⏱ box office 2-8.30pm Mon-Fri, 1hr before show Sat & Sun Ⓜ Liceu

L'Auditori (4, H2) The permanent home of Barcelona's symphony orchestra (known as OBC) is a starkly modern, and relatively new, pleasure dome for serious music lovers. Its comfortable (and acoustically unrivalled) main auditorium hosts orchestral and chamber music throughout the year as well as occasional world music jams. ☎ 93 247 93 00 🖳 www.auditori.com ✉ Carrer de Lepant 150, L'Eixample € €10-43 ⏱ box office 10am-9pm Ⓜ Marina

L'Espai (4, D3) This government-sponsored space is a showcase for the performing arts in Catalonia and concentrates on an extensive programme of contemporary dance. Classical and experimental groups also hit their straps here, and there's occasionally music without movement. ☎ 93 414 31 33 ✉ Travessera de Gràcia 63, Sant Gervasi ⏱ box office 6.30-9.30pm Tue-Sat, 5-7pm Sun Ⓜ Diagonal

Palau de la Música Catalana (5, F1) Still the main venue for classical, choral and chamber music, this Modernista masterpiece hosts an extensive concert programme encompassing everything from young, local ensembles to international orchestras. The performance space is visually stunning but acoustically inferior, although continuing renovations and extensions are improving the venue all the time.
☎ 93 295 72 00 ⌨ www.palaumusica .org ✉ Carrer de Sant Francesc de Paula 2, La Ribera ◷ box office Mon-Sat 10am-9pm, 1hr before performance Sun Ⓜ Urquinaona

Teatre Lliure (7, C2) The most prestigious theatre group working in Catalan today, this company is renowned for turning its hand to just about anything, and with flair. Expect the works, from Anglo classics to the vanguard indigenous productions. Performances are on a stage in the middle of the theatre, surrounded by the audience. The Gràcia theatre is not enough to contain the company's creative élan, and so two new stages have emerged in the **Montjuïc Teatre Lliure** (1, B1; ☎ 93 228 97 47; Plaça de Margarida Xirgu s/n; metro Espanya).
☎ 93 218 92 51 ⌨ www.teatrelliure.com ✉ Carrer del Montseny 47, Gràcia € €12-22,

Montjuïc theatre €10-16 ◷ box office 5-10pm Tue-Sun Ⓜ Fontana

Teatre Nacional de Catalunya (4, H2) Funded by the city council and designed to be the home of Catalan theatre, this expensive hi-tech venue, designed by Ricard Bofill, opened in 1997 amid controversy. Initially attacked by critics for being too commercial, it now offers a broad range of Catalan theatre, dance and a mixed bag of international performances.
☎ 93 306 57 00 ⌨ www .tnc.es, in Catalan ✉ Plaça de les Arts 1, L'Eixample € shows €15.50-22 ◷ 9pm Tue-Sat, 6pm Sun, box office 3-9pm Tue-Sat, noon-6pm Sun Ⓜ Glòries

GAY & LESBIAN BARCELONA

Aire (6, A4) Part of the Arena gay-disco chain, this is one of the most accessible lesbian dance bars in Barcelona. Sunday night is for gals only, but during the rest of the week a handful of blokes (gay or straight) tend to wander in.
☎ 93 487 83 42 ⌨ www.arenadisco.com, in Castilian ✉ Carrer de València 236, L'Eixample € free ◷ 11.30pm-3am Thu-Sat, 6-10pm Sun Ⓜ Passeig de Gràcia

Arena Madre (6, A5) Arena clubs abound in gay Barcelona, and the name is used for four different venues, all within an easy stumble of one another.

The Arena Madre, also known as just Arena, is where the young crowd goes cruising to a throbbing soundtrack of house, garage and techno. There's a long dance floor and a dark room.
☎ 93 487 49 48 ⌨ www.arenadisco.com, in Castilian ✉ Carrer de Balmes 32, L'Eixample € €5-10 ◷ Tue-Sat 12.30-5am, 7.30pm-5am Sun Ⓜ Universitat

Dietrich Gay Teatro Café (4, F4) This divinely glam corner of l'Eixample is big and friendly, and full of pretty professionals. A classic of the Gaixample, it hosts some of the best drag in the city in its elegant

quarters – all timber finishings on two levels. Quiet during the week, it goes a little wild with drag shows and dancing from Friday on.
☎ 93 451 77 07 ✉ Carrer del Consell de Cent 255, L'Eixample € free ◷ 10.30pm-3am Ⓜ Universitat

Metro (5, B1) Both dance floors of the city's biggest and busiest gay club are absolutely heaving at weekends (and on weekday theme nights) when a 90% gay crowd thumps to top-of-the-range house and techno. During the week it's dance-club pop and handbags ahoy, and is generally too gay for many. There's a dark room for those who want to get really hot under the collar.

☎ 93 323 52 27 ✉ Carrer de Sepúlveda 185, L'Eixample € €10 ☽ midnight-5am Sun-Thu, midnight-6am Fri & Sat Ⓜ Universitat

New Chaps (6, C2) As the name suggests, this bar is strictly for chaps – mostly mature, macho and suitably hirsute. It attracts a regular jean- and leather-clad posse, and has theme nights and a shadowy downstairs. You've been warned: the dungeons here are not for the faint-hearted!

☎ 93 215 53 65 ✉ Avda Diagonal 365, L'Eixample € free ☽ 9pm-3am Mon-Sat, 7pm-3am Sun Ⓜ Diagonal

Punto BCN (4, F4) This place is a classic for pre- or post-prandial drinks. Attracting a relaxed 30-something crowd of all shapes and sizes, it's extremely popular and one of the few gay meeting places that open early. A large upstairs seating area allows you to survey the talent below. Fridays are fundays, with surprises and prizes.

☎ 93 453 61 23 🖳 www .arenadisco.com, in Castilian ✉ Carrer de Muntaner 63-65, L'Eixample € free ☽ 6pm-2.30am Ⓜ Universitat

Salvation (5, F1) Flavour of the month, again, Salvation is the place for a big, happy blow-out. There are two vast dance floors offering house and chart for wiggling and watching.

The gleaming torsos of the staff are part of the attraction, but there's strictly no touching.

☎ 93 318 06 86 ✉ Ronda de Sant Pere 19-21, L'Eixample € €10 ☽ midnight-5am Fri-Sun Ⓜ Urquinaona

Sauna Casanova (4, F4) There are stacks of gay saunas dotted around the centre of the city. This one is central and can become particularly crowded, with the clientele a fairly mixed set of age groups and looks. Some of the other places tend to specialise rather more (in strapping young hairless fellas or big hairy bears, as the case may be).

☎ 93 323 78 60 ✉ Carrer de Casanova 57, L'Eixample € €3 ☽ 24hrs Ⓜ Urgell

SPORT

Football

Football is far and away the most popular spectator sport in the city, and **Football Club Barcelona** (known as Barça to most; p21), the main club, is one of the biggest in the world, with more than 112,000 official members in 2004. The side plays at the 100,000-seat **Camp Nou stadium** (4, B4; ☎ 902 189900; www.fcbarcelona.com; Carrer d'Aristides Maillol, Les Corts; tickets €30-90; ☽ box office 9am-1.30pm & 3.30-6pm Mon-Fri; metro Collblanc), and tickets for the big matches can be quite hard to come by. Touts always work the stadium, but you need to be careful, as security is tight.

Basketball

After football, basketball runs a distant second as a spectator sport. **FC Barcelona** (4, B5; ☎ 902 189900; www.fcbarcelona.com; Palau Blaugrana, Carrer d'Aristides Maillol, Les Corts; tickets €13-26; metro Collblanc) also has a winning basketball team that took the national league championship in 2004, its 13th premiership. It generally plays on Saturday afternoons.

Pillars of the Community

If you're in town when there's a *festa major* (festival) on, you may come across a curious Catalan crew known as the *castellers* (human-castle builders), who construct mobile monuments to teamwork. Teams build 'castles' by raising levels of people standing on each other's shoulders. At the base, a veritable scrum of team members helps keep the rest standing. The aim is to raise the 'castles' as high as possible, with anything from just one person per level (known as a 'pillar') to five or six. More common are towers of three or four per level. If all goes well, the *castell* is completed when an *anxaneta*, a kid with balls as big as his head, clambers to the top and gives a nervous wave to the relieved crowd, the signal to start whooping with abandon. More than 60 *colles* (teams) join in competitions and festivals throughout Catalonia. The golden age of the *castellers* was in the 1880s, when one daring team reached the record of 10 levels, a feat not repeated until 1998.

Motor Sports

The motor-racing circuit at Montmeló, 20km northeast of the city, hosts the Spanish Grand Prix in late April or early May and a motorcycle grand prix in June. Contact the **Circuit de Catalunya** (☎ 93 571 97 71; www .circuitcat.com; Carrer de Parets del Vallès) for details. Tickets for the Formula One action cost €240 to €375, depending largely on how far in advance you book. Purchase over the phone, at the track, online with ServiCaixa (p82) or at advance-sales desks in El Corte Inglés department stores. You can get a regular *rodalies* (local) train to Montmeló (€1.20, 30 minutes) but will need to walk about 3km or find a local taxi (about €8 to €10) to reach the track.

Bullfighting

Catalans generally don't like bullfighting (and the city council voted in a symbolic gesture to declare the city anti-bullfighting in early 2004), but if you must you can watch events at 6pm on Sunday during the summer months at the **Plaça Braus Monumental** (4, H2; ☎ 93 245 58 02; cnr Gran Via de les Corts Catalanes & Carrer de la Marina; metro Monumental). Tickets are available at the **arena** (⏱ 10.30am-2pm & 6-7pm Wed-Sat, 10am-6pm Sun) or through ServiCaixa (p82). You can also acquire them at **Toros Taquilla Oficial** (4, F4; Carrer de Muntaner 26; metro Universitat).

Uh-oh, he sees you…

Sleeping

The 1992 Olympics began a hotel-construction boom in Barcelona that hasn't let up since. The rapid growth in the number of available beds in the city has hardly outstripped demand, but since 2001 it has improved your chances of finding a bed at short notice (and has put a bit of a brake on spiralling room prices). Booking remains a sound idea, however, as the place remains one of Europe's favourite city destinations and has a busy trade-fair calendar.

Although La Rambla is lined with hotels in virtually all categories and is doubtless a central and engaging location, you may want to fan out. Deeper inside the Barri Gòtic are some gems, ranging from bright cheapies to gorgeously revamped old mansions. A handful of good options also lurk in the streets of El Raval and La Ribera. Spread across the generous expanse of L'Eixample is a much greater range, including many mid- to upper-range business-oriented places and some luxury classics. A couple of waterfront five-stars are tempting, too.

Room Rates
The categories indicate the cost per night of a standard double room in high season.

Deluxe	from €251
Top End	€151-250
Mid-Range	€71-150
Budget	€70 & under

At the smaller, often more personal end of the accommodation scene are the *pensiones* and *hostales*, often family-run establishments where several rooms share a bathroom in the corridor. The category of *hotel* implies the provision of several mandatory services, including *en suite* bathroom. A characterful *hostal* often appeals more than an average *hotel*. Accommodation rates are subject to a 7% value-added tax known as IVA.

If you roll into town without a reservation, head straight to the tourist office on Plaça de Catalunya (5, D1), which even at the busiest times can usually find you shelter (although during trade fairs it's tough).

There's hardly such a thing as a low season. Hotels that cater largely for professionals often offer discounts at weekends, Christmas and Easter and during the summer, when there's less business activity. Otherwise, January and February are relatively quiet times.

There are no self-esteem issues at the Hotel Majèstic (opposite)

DELUXE

Hotel Arts Barcelona
(4, J4) Barcelona's most fashionable hotel is in a skyscraper overlooking the beach. Designed by US architects Skidmore, Owings and Merrill, it is required shelter for fashion victims and style queens. The rooms are superbly equipped and decorated with original art, but the place has an impersonal atmosphere. The views, of course, are remarkable.
☎ 93 221 10 00 ☐ www .ritzcarlton.com ✉ Carrer de la Marina 19-21, Port Olímpic Ⓜ Ciutadella Vila Olímpica Ⓟ ♿ excellent ✕ Enoteca Bombaci, Arola & Café Veranda ♿

Hotel Casa Fuster (6, B1)
This sumptuous Modernista mansion at the top end of the city's showcase boulevard has been transformed into a luxury hotel. Standard rooms are plush if smallish, with nice touches such as fresh flowers. Some of the suites are remarkable. Hang about in the ground-floor piano bar, take a swim in the pool or work out in the modest gym.
☎ 902 202345 ☐ www.hotelescenter .es ✉ Passeig de Grà-cia 132 Ⓜ Diagonal ♿ good ✕ Restaurant Gourmet

Hotel Claris (6, C3) This is the best Barcelona lobby in which to pretend you're a recalcitrant rock star. Occupying a completely revamped 19th-century corner mansion that combines the grace of the past with a post-modern slickness, the hotel is also a minor museum with, among other items, several dozen exhibits from ancient Egypt. Relax by the rooftop pool after sightseeing.
☎ 93 487 62 62 ☐ www.derbyhotels.es ✉ Carrer de Pau Claris 150, L'Eixample Ⓜ Passeig de Gràcia Ⓟ ♿ excellent ✕ East 47, Restaurant Claris & La Terraza del Claris ♿

Hotel Comtes de Barcelona (6, B3) These dazzling digs occupy a revamped Modernista pile, and across the road, another more recent building. The pentagonal foyer in the main building is magnificent, the beds king-size and the baths big enough for a workout. If you stand on your tippy-toes you can see La Pedrera from the rooftop terrace.
☎ 93 467 47 80 ☐ www.hotelcondes debarcelona.com ✉ Passeig de Gràcia 73-75, L'Eixample Ⓜ Diagonal Ⓟ ♿ good ✕ Restaurante Thalassa ♿

Hotel Majèstic (6, B4)
A matter-of-fact eliteness pervades this beautiful hotel. It comprises three splendid old buildings that were knocked into one. The doubles are tasteful, large and comfortable, but the singles are a little stingy on space. The rooftop pool is great for cooling off and just admiring the views.
☎ 93 488 17 17 ☐ www.hotelmajestic.es ✉ Passeig de Gràcia 70, L'Eixample Ⓜ Passeig de Gràcia Ⓟ ♿ excellent ✕ Drolma ♿

Your Home Away from Home

A growing number of visitors are skipping the hotels altogether and opting for short-term rental apartments. The trend is catching on, and the number of available apartments is growing fast. Often the easiest way to arrange your home away from home is on the Web. As a rule, you're looking at about €40 to €60 a day for a small apartment or studio for one or two people. Bigger places can accommodate five or six people and cost from €150 a day. Search the following websites: www.barcelona-on-line.es; www.decimononico.com; www .vivebarcelona.com; www.barcelonapartments.com; www.apartmentbarcelona .com; www.bcnapart.com; www.apartime.com; www.groupbcn.com and www.oh-barcelona.com.

Hotel Omm: we're not in Kansas any more

Hotel Neri (3, A2)

Barcelona can get a little hung up on design, but here it is beautifully integrated into the old-world beauty of a centuries-old mansion in the epicentre of the old city. A combination of light, sandy stone and timber furnishings gives the 22 rooms a rustic feel. Sun and shower yourself on the roof deck.
☎ 93 304 06 55 ▯ www .hotelneri.com ✉ Carrer de Sant Sever 5, Barri Gòtic Ⓜ Jaume I ♿ good ✖ Restaurante Neri

Hotel Omm (6, B2) In a city that prides itself on such weirdness as nearby Casa Batlló and La Pedrera, the shimmering, metallic look of this design hotel comes as little surprise. Peeled back like so many strips of foil are the balcony walls, allowing you to look out but no-one to look in. A minimalist bar area dominates the foyer, and upstairs ultramodern rooms await.
☎ 93 445 40 00 ▯ www.hotelomm.es, in Castilian ✉ Carrer de Rosselló 265, L'Eixample Ⓜ Diagonal ♿ good ✖ Moo

Hotel Ritz (4, G3) Founded in 1919 by Caesar Ritz, Barcelona's classic grand hotel offers more character and old-fashioned style than all the others put together. It's a cornucopia of opulence from imperial lobby to immense and luxuriant rooms with step-down marble Roman baths.
☎ 93 318 52 00 ▯ www.ritzbcn.com ✉ Gran Via de les Corts Catalanes 668, L'Eixample Ⓜ Passeig de Gràcia Ⓟ ✖ Caelis ♿

TOP END

Hotel Axel (4, F4) Fashion and gay (check out the drag-queen show in the restaurant) are the two bywords for these sleek, corner-block digs. Rooms have plasma-screen TVs, light colour schemes and (in the double rooms) king-size beds to play in. Superior rooms have sunny enclosed galleries. The bar is a place to be seen. Take a break in the rooftop pool, the Finnish sauna or the Jacuzzi.
☎ 93 323 93 93 ▯ www.hotelaxel.com ✉ Carrer d'Aribau 33, L'Eixample Ⓜ Universitat ♿ good ✖ El Comedor del Axel

Hotel Colón (3, B1)

Housed behind a distinguished neoclassical façade on one of the city's most social spaces, this hotel offers stunning views of the Catedral. The rooms are tastefully furnished, some with dark hardwood floors, and those lucky enough to be on the top floor enjoy spacious terraces.
☎ 93 301 14 04 ▯ www.hotelcolon.es ✉ Avda de la Catedral 7, Barri Gòtic Ⓜ Jaume I ✖ La Carabela

Nightlife Versus Sleep

When you are not contributing to the racket yourself, raucous revellers, late-night garbage collection, overzealous sirens, church bells and barking dogs could all come between you and your zzzs. Where double glazing is absent in central hotels, light sleepers should consider forsaking the room with the wonderful street views in favour of (an often darker) one at the back. Earplugs can come in very handy!

Hotel Duques de Bergara (5, C1)

This hotel occupies a handsome 1898 building on a quiet street sandwiched between the old and new quarters. The foyer and stairways are original, while the rest of the interior has been completely renovated. Rooms are pleasant, and there's a pool big enough to work up a sweat in.

☎ 93 301 51 51
⌨ www.hoteles-catalonia.es ✉ Carrer de Bergara 11, L'Eixample
Ⓜ Catalunya Ⓟ ♿ fair
⊠ El Duc 🍴

Hotel Inglaterra (5, C1)

This gleaming modern hotel lacks the sombre business-conference atmosphere of many others catering to professional travellers. Designed by local boy Joan Pere, and decorated with Asian motifs and original art, it combines refined comforts with a central location. The roof terrace is ideal for an early-evening tipple.

☎ 93 505 11 00
⌨ www.hotel-inglaterra.com ✉ Carrer de Pelai 14, L'Eixample
Ⓜ Universitat ♿ fair
⊠ Restaurant-cafeteria

Hotel Oriente (5, C4)

A mouldering classic occupying part of what remains of a 17th-century monastery, the Oriente was established in 1842 as Barcelona's first grand hotel. Rooms are spacious but spartan. Though the old place is fraying a little around the edges, the wonderful public areas make these some of the most atmospheric lodgings in the city.

☎ 93 302 25 58
⌨ www.husa.es ✉ La Rambla 45 Ⓜ Drassanes, Liceu ⊠ Biblioteca

Hotel San Agustín (5, C3)

Carved out of an early-18th-century convent nextdoor to the still-functioning eponymous church, this hotel has been welcoming weary wayfarers since 1840. Rooms come with air-con, heating and satellite TV, and the top-floor rooms look out onto an expansive square. The attics have a charm all their own.

☎ 93 318 16 58
⌨ www.hotelsa.com
✉ Plaça de Sant Agustí 3, El Raval Ⓜ Liceu
♿ fair ⊠ Restaurante Hotel San Agustín

Step back in time through the portals of the Hotel Oriente

MID-RANGE

Hostal Palacios (6, B5)
Housed in a classified building, this up-market *hostal* offers some lovely rooms, with high ceilings, sun streaming through bedraped balcony doors, and old-style furnishings. The suites are extra spacious and can be taken as triples.
☎ 93 301 37 92 ⊠ La Rambla de Catalunya 27 Ⓜ Passeig de Gràcia ✕ Cerveseria Catalana

Hostal Windsor (6, B3) This is a good and inexpensive option on one of the city's loveliest *ramblas*. Singles can be a little small and dark, but the doubles are more than adequate, particularly those with views over the street. Quaint Victorianesque furnishings and mild-mannered staff give it a pleasant and welcoming vibe.
☎ 93 215 11 98 ⊠ La Rambla de Catalunya 84, L'Eixample Ⓜ Passeig de Gràcia ✕ Cerveseria Catalana

Hotel Astoria (4, E3) Just a short walk from the shopping and Modernisme of Passeig de Gràcia in a perfect uptown spot, this is a classy three-star surrounded by a host of good restaurants and bars on nearby Carrer d'Aribau. Contemporary art, a small gym and broad variety in room décor are among the features of these smart lodgings.
☎ 93 209 83 11 ⌨ www .derbyhotels.es ⊠ Carrer de París 203 Ⓜ Diagonal Ⓟ ♿ good ✕ Restaurant Astoria

Hotel Balmes (6, A3)
Run by the same crowd as the Astoria, this is another quality option a little closer to the old centre. Again, the décor varies greatly from one room to another. Among the better rooms are a few split-level options, some with private terrace. Hanging gardens cascade into the internal courtyard and pool area.
☎ 93 451 19 14 ⌨ www.derbyhotels.es ⊠ Carrer de Mallorca 216 🚇 FGC Provença Ⓟ ♿ fair ✕ Restaurant Balmes

Hotel Banys Orientals (8, A2) On what was once the city's silversmiths' street, this delightful, slender design hotel has been lovingly created within a carefully restored shell. Rooms, with parquet floors and cool colours, are a little small but great value for money.
☎ 93 268 84 60 ⌨ www.hotelbanys orientals.com ⊠ Carrer de l'Argenteria 37 Ⓜ Jaume I ✕ Senyor Parellada

Hotel California (5, D4)
One of the few hotels to openly welcome gay guests, this place has an unbeatable location in the heart of Barri Gòtic. Some of the rooms (all *en suite*) are a little grim, but the multilingual reception opens 24 hours.
☎ 93 317 77 66 ⌨ www.hotelcalifornia bcn.com ⊠ Carrer d'En Rauric 14, Barri Gòtic Ⓜ Liceu ✕ La Cereria

Hotel Continental (5, D2)
If you're looking forward to getting stuck into George Orwell's *Homage to Catalonia*, where better than the place the author recovered from a bullet wound? Space is scarce in most of the rooms, but some have semicircular balconies with wonderful views over the lively Rambla.
☎ 93 301 25 70 ⌨ www.hotelcontinen tal.com ⊠ La Rambla 138 Ⓜ Catalunya ✕ Els Quatre Gats

Hotel D'Uxelles (4, G3)
A charming simplicity pervades the 14 rooms here. Wrought-iron bedheads are decked in flowing drapes, room décor varies (from blues and whites to beige-and-cream combos), and some rooms have little terraces. Get a back room, as the Gran Via is incredibly noisy.
☎ 93 265 35 60 ⌨ www.hotelduxelles .com/principal2ingles.htm ⊠ Gran Via de les Corts Catalanes 688 Ⓜ Tetuan ✕ Casa Calvet

Hotel España (5, C4) If Modernisme means more to you than comfort, head to this landmark hotel, the lower floors of which were designed by Domènech i Montaner and decorated by celebrated artisans of the era. The dining rooms are magnificent, but the guest rooms are functional and drab.
☎ 93 318 17 58 ⌨ hotel espanya@tresnet.com ⊠ Carrer de Sant Pau 9-11, El Raval Ⓜ Liceu ✕ Hotel España

Hotel Gran Via (6, C6) This place oozes old-fashioned charm, and much of its 19th-century interior remains intact. Guest rooms have been comfortably tweaked, but the public areas (complete with antique furnishings) retain the grace of another age, and there's a wonderful courtyard in which to relax after a long day.
☎ 93 318 19 00
🖥 www.nnhotels.es
✉ Gran Via de les Corts Catalanes 642, L'Eixample
Ⓜ Passeig de Gràcia
Ⓟ ♿ good ✗ Casa Calvet

Hotel Hispanos Siete Suiza (4, G2) Near the towering madness of the Sagrada Família, you wander through a modest entrance to take up residence in one of 18 generous apartments, all of which have two double rooms, separate bathrooms, a lounge, a kitchen and a terrace. Parked amid the tables of the hotel's excellent La Cúpula restaurant are several gleaming Hispano-Suiza cars of 1920s manufacture.
☎ 93 208 20 51
🖥 www.hispanos7suiza .com ✉ Carrer de Sicilia 255, L'Eixample Ⓜ Sagrada Família Ⓟ ♿ fair ✗ La Cúpula

Hotel Jardí (5, D3) The best rooms are the doubles overlooking the picturesque square (especially the top-floor ones). The better rooms are bright and reasonable (and awfully popular), the service generally leaves a lot to be desired, and some of the back rooms are nothing special.
☎ 93 301 59 00; fax 93 318 36 64 ✉ Plaça de Sant Josep Oriol 1, Barri Gòtic Ⓜ Liceu ✗ Attic

Hotel Mesón de Castilla (5, B1) This hotel feels more country than city, thanks to its warm staff and soothing atmosphere. The rooms are gracefully furnished, the public areas are congenial, with Modernista features, and the interior patio is a delightful place to start the day by tucking into a hearty buffet breakfast.
☎ 93 318 21 82
🖥 www.husa.es
✉ Carrer de Valldonzella 5, El Raval Ⓜ Universitat ✗ Bar Kasparo

Hotel Onix Rambla (6, B5) Forty modern rooms are spread through this former urban mansion just a few steps away from Plaça de Catalunya. Rooms are simple enough but fully equipped, and pluses include a small outdoor pool, a solarium and a handful of exercise machines.
☎ 93 342 79 80
🖥 www.hotelsonix .com ✉ La Rambla de Catalunya 24, L'Eixample Ⓜ Catalunya Ⓟ ✗ Cerveseria Catalana

Park Hotel (5, G4) Welcome to retro. This 1950s hotel, oozing details of that period such as the sea-green tiles and angular spiral stairway, continues to be refurbished with painstaking care. Dark wood and fabrics dominate the renovated rooms, some of which have terraces. Those still not done up are not so hot. You are a short stroll from the Port Vell marina and the merriment of El Born.
☎ 93 319 60 00
🖥 www.parkhotel barcelona.com, in Castilian ✉ Avinguda del Marquès de l'Argentera 11, La Ribera Ⓜ Barceloneta Ⓟ ✗ Àbac

The congenial Hotel Mesón de Castilla

BUDGET

Alberg Mare de Déu de Montserrat (4, D1) This 220-place hostel is 4km north of the centre. The main building is a magnificent former mansion with a Mudéjar-style lobby. Most rooms sleep six.
☎ 93 210 51 51
🖳 www.tujuca.com
✉ Passeig de la Mare de Déu del Coll 41-51
Ⓜ Vallcarca ♿ good
✗ hostal restaurant

Hostal Central (6, A6) This place is spread over several renovated flats. Some of the larger rooms have charming enclosed terraces looking onto the (admittedly noisy) street. Mosaic and parquet floors and some nice decorative touches make it an attractive option.
☎ 93 302 24 20
🖳 hostalcentral@wana doo.es ✉ Ronda de l'Universitat 11, L'Eixample
Ⓜ Universitat
✗ Bar Kasparo

Hostal Gat Raval (5, B2) They've opted for a pea-green and lemon-lime colour scheme in this hip young *hostal* on the 2nd floor in one of the grittier lanes of El Raval. Rooms are pleasant and secure, and each is behind a green door, but only some have their own bathroom. All have TV and some enjoy views across to the bright white Macba contemporary art museum.
☎ 93 481 66 70
🖳 www.gataccom modation.com ✉ Carrer de Joaquín Costa 44, El

Raval Ⓜ Universitat
✗ Elisabets

Hostal Levante (5, D4) Off Plaça de Sant Miquel, this large, bright *hostal* has rooms of all shapes and sizes. Try for a double with a balcony. You may be walking in the footsteps of greatness, as the building was reputedly a house of sinful pleasure that attracted the attention of Pablo Picasso on more than one occasion. The owners have some apartments nearby.
☎ 93 317 95 65
🖳 www.hostallevante .com ✉ Baixada de Sant Miquel 2, Barri Gòtic
Ⓜ Liceu, Jaume I
✗ La Cereria

Hostal Oliva (6, C5) A picturesque antique lift wheezes its way up to this 4th-floor hostel, a terrific cheapie in one of the city's most expensive neighbourhoods. Some of the singles are barely big enough to accommodate a bed, but the doubles are large, light and airy, and several have fabulous views over Barce-

lona's grandest street.
☎ 93 488 01 62; fax 93 488 17 89 ✉ Passeig de Gràcia 32, L'Eixample
Ⓜ Passeig de Gràcia
✗ Ciudad Condal

Hotel Peninsular (5, C4) Once part of a convent, this wonderful little hotel on the fringe of the Barri Xinès has clean, spacious and economic rooms set along curved balconies overlooking a vast, plant-lined atrium.
☎ 93 302 31 38; fax 93 412 36 99 ✉ Carrer de Sant Pau 34, El Raval
Ⓜ Liceu ✗ Organic

Pensió 2000 (5, F2) This cheerful, simple place sits on the 1st floor right opposite the Modernista Palau de la Música Catalana. It has just seven reasonably spacious doubles, two with *en suite* bathroom and all with mosaic tiled floors. Eat breakfast in the little courtyard.
☎ 93 310 74 66
🖳 www.pensio2000.com
✉ Carrer de Sant Pere més Alt 6 Ⓜ Urquinaona
✗ Els Quatre Gats ♿

Breakfast Included
Many hotels include breakfast in their rates, but this is not always good news. Where a generous buffet is on offer it can be a hearty way to start the day, but often the deal can be little better than a miserable cold bun. In any event, it's generally both better value and a whole lot more fun to head out to a local café to start your day. In those places where breakfast is an optional extra, consider skipping it and going it alone.

About Barcelona

HISTORY
From Roman Town to Medieval Empire

It wasn't until the Romans turned up late in the 3rd century BC that the city of Barcino began to emerge. After short visits by the Visigoths and the Moors, it was taken over by the Franks in the 9th century AD and put under the control of local counts as a buffer zone against Muslim-dominated Spain.

Count Guifré el Pelós (Wilfred the Hairy) gained control over several territories in what later became known as Catalonia, and by 878 Barcelona was its key city. He founded a dynasty that lasted nearly five centuries. After the Franks failed to come to Barcelona's aid to repel a Muslim assault in 985, the region became independent of Frankish suzerainty.

In later centuries the counts of Barcelona expanded their territory south, expelling the Muslims from what is now southern Catalonia. In 1137 the Count of Barcelona, Ramon Berenguer IV, married Petronilla, heiress to the throne of neighbouring Aragón, and thus created the combined Crown of Aragón, which in the following centuries became a flourishing merchant empire, seizing Valencia and the Balearic Islands from the Muslims and later taking territories as far flung as Sardinia, Sicily and parts of Greece.

> **Les Quatre Barres**
> Catalonia's flag (four horizontal red stripes on a gold background) is among the oldest in Europe. It grew out of the coat of arms of the Counts of Barcelona, in which the stripes are vertical. The earliest records of it date to 1150, but its origins lie shrouded in mystery. Medieval tales of derring-do recount that Frankish king Charles the Bald found a wounded Guifré el Pelós on the battlefield with a bare golden shield. Moved by the count's bravery and surprised by his lack of coat-of-arms, he created one on the spot by dipping his fingers into Guifré's blood and dragging them down the golden shield.

Castilian Dominance

Overstretched, racked by civil disobedience and decimated by the Black Death, Catalonia began to wobble by the 14th century. When the last count of Wilfred the Hairy's dynasty died without leaving an heir, the Crown of Aragón was passed to a noble of Castile. Soon these two Spanish kingdoms were merged, and Catalonia was left on the outer. As business shifted from the Mediterranean to the Atlantic with the discovery and exploration of the Americas from 1492 on, Catalans were increasingly marginalised from trade. Castile boomed, while Catalonia declined.

The region was further weakened by revolts over the next centuries. The Reapers' War of 1640, sparked when peasant farmers murdered the viceroy, eventually saw Catalonia lose its territory north of the Pyrenees to France. Catalonia also backed the wrong side in the War of the Spanish Succession (1702–13) and paid the price when the Bourbon king, Felipe V, established a unitary Castilian state. He banned the writing and teaching of Catalan, and built a huge fort (on the site of the Parc de la Ciutadella) to watch over Barcelona's troublemakers.

Economic Growth & the Renaixença

Buoyed by the lifting of the ban on trade with the Americas in 1778, Barcelona embarked on the road to industrial revolution, based initially on textiles but spreading to wine, cork and iron in the mid-19th century. As the economy prospered, Barcelona outgrew its medieval walls, which were demolished in 1854. Work on l'Eixample (the Extension) district began soon after. The 1888 Universal Exhibition gave Barcelona a little world attention at a time when Catalans themselves were rediscovering their roots. The so-called Renaixença (Renaissance) brought a revival of Catalan culture and sowed the seeds of growing political tension in the early 20th century as demands for autonomy from the central state became more insistent.

Anarchy, Civil War & Franco

Adding to the fiery mix was growing discontent among the working class. While the grand Catalan merchant-bourgeois families grew richer (and displayed their wealth in a slew of fanciful private mansions built with verve and flair by Modernista architects such as Antoni Gaudí), the industrial working class, housed in cramped quarters and oppressed by poverty and disease, became organised and on occasion violent. Spain's neutrality during WWI had boosted Barcelona's economy, and from 1900 to 1930 the population doubled to one million, but the postwar global slump hit the city hard. Waves of strikes, organised principally by the anarchists' Confederación Nacional del Trabajo (CNT), brought tough responses. Left-wing and right-wing gangs took their ideological conflict to the streets, and the death toll mounted.

When the Second Spanish Republic was created under a left-wing government in 1931, Catalonia declared virtual independence. Later, under pressure, its leaders settled for devolution,

Did You Know?
- Population: 1.6 million
- Catalonia unemployment: 8.9%
- The resident foreign population of Barcelona doubled to 12.6% of the total from 2001 to 2003
- The greater Barcelona area exports more than Madrid, Valencia and Zaragoza combined
- Despite excellent public transport, there is almost one vehicle on the road for every inhabitant
- Women outnumber men in Barcelona by 80,000

Beam them down, Scotty: the site of the 1992 Olympics and the 2092 Intergalactic Games

which it then lost in 1934, when a right-wing government won power in Madrid. The election of a left-wing popular front in 1936 again sparked Catalan autonomy but also led General Franco to launch the 1936–39 Spanish Civil War, from which he emerged the victor. Barcelona, which for much of the war was the acting capital of Spain, fell in January 1939.

Franco was reviled in Catalonia, and the first two decades of his reign were one of the bleakest periods in Barcelona's modern history. All things Catalan were suppressed, the city was overcrowded and impoverished, and anyone who didn't toe the line was brutally punished. It wasn't until the late 1950s that Barcelona regained the standard of living it had enjoyed pre-Franco.

Barcelona Becomes Cool

When Franco died in 1975, the city rejoiced. Two years later, Catalonia was again granted regional autonomy. All the creative energy that had been bottled up in the preceding decades popped like so many bottles of *cava* (Spanish sparkling wine). The 1992 Olympics marked the beginning of a long process of urban renewal after decades of neglect. The waterfront and Montjuïc were in the first wave, but the momentum hasn't been lost since. The old city is slowly being spruced up, and a determined campaign to repair the city's façades is lending Barcelona a brighter feel. Ambitious projects like the 22@ hi-tech zone in the El Poblenou district and the fancy Diagonal Mar waterfront development at the northeast tip of the city are just two examples of Barcelona's urban dynamism. By the mid-1990s Barcelona had been 'discovered' by the rest of the world and has become one of the hippest city destinations in Europe.

ENVIRONMENT

While Barcelona isn't spared the air pollution common among crowded Mediterranean conurbations, you won't find it overwhelmingly uncomfortable. Indeed, statistics show that air pollution has been halved since the late 1980s. Much of the old centre is traffic free, and buses running on natural gas are gradually replacing their diesel-fuelled counterparts. On those days when the smog is bad, a trip to the beaches (which are pleasant enough) or the hills is a recommended tonic.

Folks line up to see the sights in Barcelona

Every night the streets are washed down by the city's cleaning department. What is extraordinary is that by evening of the following day it seems like nothing has happened. In the old centre especially, a combination of burst rubbish bags, human urine and dog doings lends the streets special odours they could do without!

Vocal late-night revellers, bongos in city squares, the high-pitched rattle of countless motor scooters, the nightly rubbish collection and street cleaning, and general city-centre traffic all combine to send the decibels soaring in Barcelona – this is not a quiet city.

GOVERNMENT & POLITICS

Barcelonins are as sceptical about their politicians as anyone else in Spain, but the politics of Catalan separatism keep plenty of spirits on the boil.

The Ajuntament (city hall) and the Generalitat (regional government) face each other across the medieval Plaça de Sant Jaume in the heart of

---

Dos & Don'ts

While 'please' and 'thank you' are the first priority in politeness in some countries, Barcelonins tend to be rather more direct, simply demanding, in bars for instance, that they be given their favourite tipple. On the other hand, it is customary when entering shops to wish all and sundry a hearty 'hola' and bid them 'adeu' upon leaving.

Men and women, and women and women, greet each other, even the first time, with a glancing kiss on each cheek, right then left.

Smokers puff to their hearts' content pretty much anywhere (except on public transport).

Be wary of getting involved in discussions about local politics. Outsiders' opinions (even if informed) are rarely accepted with good grace on the divisive subjects of greater autonomy for Catalonia and the more radical demands of some for secession.

Primary colours: the Catalan, Spanish and Barcelonin flags fly proudly over the Generalitat

the Barri Gòtic. Since its resurrection in 1977, the Generalitat has had considerable powers devolved to it by Madrid, covering local police, health, education, tourism and more.

Barcelona has traditionally been red, and the Socialist-run Ajuntament had lived uneasily with the conservative Catalan nationalist governments of one Jordi Pujol across the square for 23 years until Pujol stepped down and his government was ousted by a Socialist-led left-wing coalition under former mayor Pascual Maragall in 2003.

The most extraordinary result of the 2003 elections was the meteoric rise of the independence-minded Esquerra Republicana de Catalunya (ERC; Republican Left of Catalunya) party, led by the ambitious Josep-Lluís Carod-Rovira. The ERC holds the balance of power in the Generalitat, and Carod-Rovira has made no secret of his ambition to become the next regional president in 2007.

ECONOMY

Barcelona, the chief commercial and industrial centre of Spain, has a reputation for being a hard-working, mercantile city. The roots of its trading culture lie in the days of Mediterranean empire building, but industry first stirred to life in the small-scale textile factories that emerged late in the 18th century and helped to propel the 19th-century industrial revolution. After long being the country's economic powerhouse, there are signs that Barcelona today is losing its competitive edge. Multinationals tend to choose Madrid as their base, and inward investment in Catalonia is down.

Still, around 25% of Spanish exports come from Catalonia (mainly in and around Barcelona). Textiles and other manufacturing industries are big business, along with finance and tourism. The latter is crucial – nearly four million visitors a year flock to the port city and represent 14% of the city's GDP.

SOCIETY & CULTURE

Catalans have a reputation for being reserved but, considering the number of tourists swarming over the city centre, its people are for the most part extraordinarily tolerant and courteous. As you can tell by all the activity in the streets, especially Thursday to Saturday nights, Barcelonins are no stay-at-homes. They generally like to eat late and party later, although many prefer to escape the city altogether. Lucky folk have a second residence on the coast or in the country, and the city's main arteries can become clogged on Friday and Sunday nights as traffic streams away and back.

People do not expect you to speak Catalan or Castellano (Spanish), although they will warm to you much more quickly if you can tickle their ears with a word or two of either. One thing sure to annoy a Catalan is assuming that they speak English. Make the effort to learn a few basic phrases.

The influx of immigrants from poorer parts of Spain during the mid-20th century broadened the social make-up of the city. However, you'll generally get along better with everyone if you get into the habit of referring to 'Catalonia' rather than 'Spain'.

ARTS
Architecture

Think of architecture and Barcelona, and it's usually Gaudí who springs to mind. But Barcelona is one of Europe's great Gothic treasure chests, and it was largely from these jewels that the Modernistas of the late 19th and early 20th centuries took their inspiration, adapting the old rules and techniques to fit their new ways of seeing and building.

Apart from some Roman leftovers and Romanesque relics, Barcelona's architectural personality truly begins with its version of the Gothic style that emerged in Europe in the 13th century. This style, Catalan Gothic, took its own unique course. Decoration was used more sparingly than elsewhere but, most significantly, the Catalan builders championed breadth over height. Stunning examples include the Palau Reial's **Saló del Tinell** (p13), the **Drassanes** (the former shipyards that now house the Museu Marítim, see p22) and the glorious **Església de Santa Maria del Mar** (p12).

The Palau Reial's modest façade

Going for Gaudí

Among the young Antoni Gaudí's first jobs were contributions to the **Cascada** (waterfall) in the **Parc de la Ciutadella** (p25) and some of the lampposts in **Plaça Reial** (5, D4) in the Barri Gòtic. His main patron, magnate Eusebi Güell, had him raise the **Palau Güell** (p26) mansion in El Raval, sober in parts but utterly loopy in others – such as the kaleidoscopic chimneypots. Güell also had him design what became the city's most emblematic park – **Parc Güell** (p20). Two extraordinary private homes, **La Pedrera** (p16) and **Casa Batlló** (p17), virtually across the road from each other, testify to his fervent imagination. His life project, however, still isn't finished. The soaring, other-worldly church **La Sagrada Família** (p8) remains a unique and controversial work in progress.

Six impossible things before breakfast: the rooftop of Gaudí's La Pedrera

Modernisme (Art Nouveau) emerged as a trend in Barcelona during the 1880s, the city's *belle époque*. While the name suggests a rejection of the old, the pioneers of the style actually delved deep into the past for inspiration, absorbed everything they could and then ripped up the rulebook.

Today the movement, which began to splutter to a close in 1910, is for many people synonymous with the name **Antoni Gaudí** (1852–1926). His works (starting with the unfinished Sagrada Família church, see p8) are the most daring and well known, but Gaudí was by no means alone. **Lluís Domènech i Montaner** (1850–1923) and **Josep Puig i Cadafalch** (1867–1957) also left a wealth of remarkable buildings across the city and beyond. They range from Domènech i Montaner's gorgeous **Palau de la Música Catalana** (p24) to Puig i Cadafalch's playful medieval Dutch–looking **Casa Amatller** (p39) on Passeig de Gràcia. The many differences between each of these structures and any of Gaudí's designs underline just how eclectic and individual the Modernisme movement was.

Painting

While there might not be much Romanesque architecture still standing in Barcelona, the city has the world's best collection of paintings from the period. A great many anonymous artists left their work behind in the chapels and churches of medieval Catalonia, mostly in the form of murals and altarpieces, which depict religious figures with an ethereal aura. Much of this work was salvaged and can be seen today in the **Museu Nacional d'Art de Catalunya** (MNAC; p11), also a fine repository of Catalan Gothic art.

Ramón Casas (1866–1932) was the best-known artist to emerge from the Modernisme period in Barcelona, but he was soon to be overshadowed by the genius of **Pablo Picasso** (1881–1973). Born in Málaga in Spain's south, Picasso spent his teenage years in Barcelona in the company of the Modernistas. By the time he moved to Paris in 1904, he had already explored his first personal style in the so-called Blue Period. He went on to experiment with Cubism and become one of the greatest artists of the 20th century.

Continuing the burst of brilliance was the Barcelona-born surrealist **Joan Miró** (1893–1983), who is best remembered for his use of symbolic figures in primary colours. Hot on his heels was the delirious **Salvador Dalí** (1904–89). The artist spent precious little time in Barcelona but he deserves a mention because his monument to his own nuttiness, the **Teatre-Museu Dalí** (p49), is merely an excursion away in Figueres. **Antoni Tàpies** (1923–) is the most important artist working in Barcelona today. One of the best places to take the pulse of contemporary art in Catalonia is the **Museu d'Art Contemporani de Barcelona** (Macba; p28).

I told you this wasn't the airport – the Museu d'Art Contemporani de Barcelona

Directory

ARRIVAL & DEPARTURE 112
Air 112
Bus 112
Train 112
Boat 113
Travel Documents 113
Customs & Duty Free 113
Left Luggage 113

GETTING AROUND 113
Travel Passes 113
Metro 113
FGC 114
Bus 114
Taxi 114
Car & Motorcycle 114
Bicycle 115

PRACTICALITIES 115
Business Hours 115
Climate & When to Go 115
Disabled Travellers 115
Discounts 115
Electricity 116
Embassies & Consulates 116
Emergencies 116

Fitness 116
Gay & Lesbian Travellers 117
Health 117
Holidays 118
Internet 118
Lost Property 118
Metric System 119
Money 119
Newspapers & Magazines 119
Post 119
Radio 120
Telephone 120
Television 120
Time 121
Tipping 121
Tourist Information 121
Women Travellers 121

LANGUAGE 121
Basics 121
Getting Around 122
Accommodation 122
Around Town 122
Eating 122
Time, Days & Numbers 122
Health 122
Emergencies 122

A groundswell of art in El Raval

ARRIVAL & DEPARTURE

Barcelona is well connected with the rest of Spain and Europe by air, road, rail and sea.

Air

Most flights arrive at **Aeroport del Prat – Barcelona** (2, B3), 12km southwest of the city centre. Some low-cost airlines, including Ryanair, use Girona airport, 80km north of Barcelona.

AEROPORT DEL PRAT – BARCELONA
Information
General inquiries &
  flight information   ☎ 93 298 38 38

Airport Access
Bus The **A1 Aerobús** (☎ 93 415 60 20; €3.45; 30-40 mins) service runs from the airport to Plaça de Catalunya, stopping at Plaça d'Espanya, every 12 minutes from 6am (6.30am at weekends and on holidays) to midnight Monday to Friday. Departures from Plaça de Catalunya are from 5.30am to 11.30pm Monday to Friday (from 6am at weekends and on holidays).

Train Renfe's *rodalies* (local trains; *cercanías* in Castilian) run from the airport to several city stops, including ones at Estació Sants, Catalunya, Passeig de Gràcia, Arc de Triomf and Clot. A one-way ticket costs €2.25 (unless you have a multiride ticket for Barcelona public transport; see Travel Passes opposite). Trains run every 30 minutes from 6.13am to 11.15pm daily.

Taxi A taxi to or from the centre – about a half-hour ride depending on traffic – costs €18 to €20.

Car Parking is available at each terminal (from €1.30 an hour; maximum €9.25 a day)

GIRONA AIRPORT
Information
General inquiries &
  flight information   ☎ 972 186600

Airport Access
Bus The **Barcelona Bus** (☎ 902 361550) service runs to Girona's main bus and train station (€1.65, 20 minutes) in connection with flights. Direct Barcelona Bus services to and from Passeig de Sant Joan 52 (4, G3) in Barcelona (one way/return €9/16, 70 minutes) also connect with flights.

Taxi A taxi into Girona from the airport costs around €15. From there regular trains run between Girona and Barcelona (€5 to €5.75, 1¼ hours).

Car Free parking is available, although fees will probably be imposed as air traffic grows.

Bus

The main intercity bus station is **Estació del Nord** (4, H3; ☎ 902 260606; www.barcelonanord.com; Carrer d'Ali Bei 80; Ⓜ Arc de Triomf). Long-distance international services (and buses to Montserrat) leave from Estació d'Autobusos de Sants (4, D5) beside the main railway station, Estació Sants, but many of these also stop at Estació del Nord.

Major international carriers include **Eurolines** (☎ 902 405040, 93 490 40 00; www.eurolines.es, in Castilian), **Alsa Internacional** (☎ 902 422242; www.alsa.es) and **Linebús** (☎ 902 260606, 93 265 07 00).

Train

Virtually all long-distance trains run by the Spanish state railway **Renfe** (☎ 902 240202; www .renfe.es) use Estació Sants (4, D5; metro Sants Estació). Trains run to most Spanish cities, and there is a mind-boggling array of fare options.

If you're coming from the UK, contact the **Rail Europe Travel Centre** (☎ 08705 848 848; www .raileurope.co.uk; 179 Piccadilly, London W1). Overnight sleepers known as *trenhoteles* connect Barcelona with Paris, along with various other services.

Estació Sants has a **consigna** (left-luggage office; small/large locker 24 hr €3/4.50; ☯ 5.30am-11pm), a tourist office, currency exchange booths and ATMs.

Boat
Grandi Navi Veloci (in Italy ☎ 010 209 45 91, in Spain ☎ 902 410200; www1.gnv.it) runs modern cruise ferries from Genoa (Italy) to Barcelona three times a week. The boats dock at Moll de San Beltran (4, G6).

Ferries to and from the Balearic Islands, operated by **Trasmediter-ránea** (☎ 902 454645; www.tras mediterranea.es), dock around the Moll de Barcelona in Port Vell (4, G6).

Travel Documents
PASSPORT
If you need a visa for Spain, your passport must be valid for several months after the date of entry. EU, Swiss and Norwegian citizens only need to pack a passport or national ID card.

VISA
Nationals of Australia, Canada, Japan, New Zealand and the USA don't need a visa if they are entering as tourists for up to 90 days. Other nationals and those wishing to stay for longer periods or for work or study may need a visa. Spain is part of the Schengen accords, which means that a visa for Spain is valid for the other participating European countries.

Customs & Duty Free
If you've paid the duty, you're allowed to bring in the equivalent of 800 cigarettes, 10L of spirits, 90L of wine and 110L of beer. Check with your home country on what you're allowed to bring back. Arrivals from outside the EU are allowed to bring in 200 cigarettes, 50 cigars or 250g of tobacco, 1L of spirits and 2L of wine duty free.

Left Luggage
Left luggage (*consigna*; open 24 hours) at Aeroport del Prat is on the ground floor at the end of Terminal B closest to Terminal C. Each terminal has a lost-luggage office on the arrivals floor if your bags don't appear. There is no left-luggage service at Girona airport.

GETTING AROUND
Barcelona has a very user-friendly transport system. The efficient metro stops close to most places of interest and is complemented by the suburban rail system Ferrocarrils de la Generalitat de Catalunya (FGC) and an extensive bus network. In this book, the nearest metro/bus/FGC stations or routes are noted after the Ⓜ / 🚌 / 🚆 symbols in each listing.

Travel Passes
Targetas are multiple-trip tickets that will save you time and money and are sold at most metro stations. T-10 (€6) gives you 10 trips on the metro, buses and FGC trains. T-DIA (€4.60) gives unlimited travel on all transport for one day. Two-/three-/four-/five-day tickets for unlimited travel on all transport except *rodalies* (local trains) cost €8.40/11.80/15.20/18.20.

Metro
The metro has six efficient, colour-coded lines. Single tickets, good for one journey no matter how many

changes you have to make, cost €1.10. The metro operates from 5am to midnight Monday to Thursday, until 2am Friday and Saturday (and the day before public holidays), and 6am to midnight on Sunday.

FGC

This suburban network (☎ 93 205 15 15; www.fgc.net) will come in handy for trips from Plaça de Catalunya to scattered attractions such as Tibidabo and Pedralbes. It operates on the same schedule as the metro.

Bus

Most buses run between 6am and as late as 11pm (depending on the line) Monday to Thursday and until 2am Friday, Saturday and the days before holidays. Afterwards a reduced schedule of yellow *nit-busos* (night buses) operates until anything from 3am to 5am. Single tickets are €1.10.

Taxi

Barcelona's black-and-yellow cabs are reasonably priced and can be hailed when a green light on the roof shows that they are *lliure/libre* (free). Taxis charge €1.20 flagfall (€1.35 from 10pm to 6am weekdays and all day Saturday, Sunday and holidays) plus meter charges of €0.71 per kilometre (€0.91). A further €2.10 is added for all trips to/from the airport, and €0.85 for luggage bigger than 55cm x 35cm x 35cm. The trip from Estació Sants to Plaça de Catalunya, about 3km, costs roughly €5. You can call a taxi (☎ 93 225 00 00, 93 300 11 00 or 93 303 30 33) or flag them down in the streets.

Car & Motorcycle

With the combination of a complex one-way system, impatient drivers, the possibility of theft and slim hopes of finding a parking space, you're better off using public transport than driving your own vehicle. It's common to race through amber lights so be careful before braking at these or you might get rear-ended.

HIRE

Avis (☎ 902 135531), **Europcar** (☎ 902 105030), **Hertz** (☎ 902 402405) and several other big companies have offices in Barcelona, and desks at the airport, Estació Sants train station and Estació del Nord bus terminus. An interesting budget operation is **Pepecar** (5, D1; ☎ 807 212121; www.pepecar.com; Plaça de Catalunya; metro Catalunya). Generally cheaper than the big companies, depending on how far ahead you book, it also has outlets near the airport and in Carrer de Béjar 68 (4, D5), near Sants train station.

ROAD RULES

Spaniards drive on the right, and the wearing of seat belts is compulsory. In built-up areas the speed limit is 50km/hr; it scales up to 120km/hr on motorways. The blood-alcohol limit when driving is 0.05%.

Parking is tough. As a general guide: red markings mean not on your life, blue mean pay and display, and yellow mean you can park for up to half an hour if you're loading and unloading. Tickets and tows are common, especially during working hours Monday to Saturday.

If you get towed, call the **Dipòsit Municipal** (vehicle pound; ☎ 902 364116). Depending on the place your car was nabbed, you will be directed to one of several pounds around town. You pay €100.60 for the tow and €1.60 per hour (maximum of €16 per day).

DRIVING LICENCE & PERMIT

Bring with you either an EU driving licence or an International Driving Permit, plus your home-country licence.

Bicycle

Several bicycle-hire outfits operate in central Barcelona. CicloBus (run by the city public-transport agency) allows you to hire a bike in one spot and return it at another (one hour/half day/day/weekend €4.50/11/15/21). The hire spots are Plaça de Catalunya, Monument a Colom and Estació Sants. The service operates from 10am to 8pm daily, April to September and from 10am to 6pm daily October to March.

PRACTICALITIES
Business Hours

Generally, people work Monday to Friday from 8am or 9am to 2pm and then again from 4.30pm or 5pm for another three hours.

Banks tend to open 8.30am to 2pm Monday to Friday. Some open again from around 4pm to 7pm on Thursday evenings and/or Saturday mornings from around 9am to 1pm. The central post office opens 8.30am to 9.30pm Monday to Saturday and 9am to 2pm on Sunday. Some branches open 8.30am to 8.30pm Monday to Friday and 9.30am to 1pm Saturday, but most open only 8am to 2pm, Monday to Friday.

Typical restaurant hours are about 1pm to 4pm and 8pm to midnight. You can generally linger later, but most kitchens close by these times. Most places close one day a week.

Climate & When to Go

Barcelona's Mediterranean climate brings cool winters and hot summers. In July and much of August, the heat and humidity can be torrid, with temperatures sometimes nudging 37°C. From January to March, temperatures can plummet to a crisp 5°C. Late April and May are pleasant times to visit, as are September and early October

if you're lucky enough to avoid the late-summer thunderstorms. Locals abandon the city in August, when many restaurants (among other things) close. It's good to be in town for the Festes de la Mercè (p118).

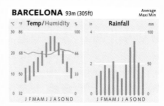

Disabled Travellers

Some hotels, monuments and public institutions have wheelchair access. All metro stations and buses should be wheelchair adapted by 2007 (in 2004 only about 12% of metro stops were fully accessible).

INFORMATION & ORGANISATIONS

The **Institut Municipal de Persones amb Disminució** (4, H2; ☎ 93 413 27 75; Avinguda Diagonal 233) can provide information for disabled people in Barcelona, but it is aimed mostly at permanent residents. **ONCE** (4, E5; ☎ 93 325 92 00; Carrer de Calàbria 66-76; metro Rocafort), the national blind people's organisation, has a guide to Barcelona in Braille.

Discounts

Articket (p7) and Barcelona Card each offer discounted entry to some sights. The Barcelona Card costs €17/20/23/25/27 for 1/2/3/4/5 days. You get free transport and up to 100% off admission prices to many museums and other sights, as well as minor discounts at a limited number of shops, restaurants and bars. The card is available at the tourist offices. Other tickets worth looking for include the Ruta del Modernisme ticket (p40) and the Montjuïc Card (p29).

STUDENT & YOUTH CARDS

The **ISIC** (International Student Identity Card; www.isic.org) and the **Euro26 card** (for youth under 26; www.euro26.org) are available from most national student organisations and can gain you discounted access to sights.

SENIORS' CARDS

With appropriate ID, people 65 or over can get discounted admission to many attractions.

Electricity

Voltage	220V
Frequency	50Hz
Cycle	AC
Plugs	standard continental two round pins

Embassies & Consulates

Most countries have an embassy in Madrid. Look them up under *Embajada* in that city's Paginas Amarillas (Yellow Pages). Various countries maintain consulates in Barcelona. They include:

Australia (4, C4; ☎ 93 490 90 13; 9th fl, Gran Via de Carles III 98; metro Maria Cristina)

Canada (4, B2; ☎ 93 204 27 00; Carrer d'Elisenda de Pinós 10; FGC Reina Elisenda)

France (6, B6; ☎ 93 270 30 00; Ronda de l'Universitat 22B; metro Catalunya)

Germany (6, B1; ☎ 93 292 10 00; Passeig de Gràcia 111; metro Diagonal)

Ireland (4, C4; ☎ 93 491 50 21; Gran Via de Carles III 94; metro Maria Cristina)

New Zealand (4, E3; ☎ 93 209 03 99; Travessera de Gràcia 64; FGC Gràcia)

UK (4, D3; ☎ 93 366 62 00; Avinguda Diagonal 477; metro Hospital Clínic)

USA (4, B3; ☎ 93 280 02 95; Passeig de la Reina Elisenda de Montcada 23-25; FGC Reina Elisenda)

Emergencies

Ambulance	☎ 061
EU standard emergency number	☎ 112
Fire brigade	☎ 080, 085
Guàrdia Urbana (local police)	☎ 092
Policía Nacional (national police)	☎ 091

Fitness

There's no shortage of ways to keep fit in Barcelona. You can go for a bracing early-morning dip in the sea or treat yourself to a little in-line skating along the waterfront. Joggers can join the skaters, or head up to Montjuïc or the Parc de Collserola. The latter is also good for some strenuous mountain-bike activity. Work out in one of the city's gyms or do some laps at a pool.

GYMS & HEALTH CLUBS

DIR (6, B3; ☎ 93 488 08 09; www .dir.es, in Castilian; Passatge del Domingo 6-8; 7 consecutive days €30.45; ⊙ 7am-11pm Mon-Fri, 9am-3pm Sat, Sun & hols; metro Passeig de Gràcia) A chain of fitness clubs with branches all over town (general information ☎ 901 304030).

UBAE Frontón (5, D5; ☎ 93 302 32 95; La Rambla de Santa Mònica 18; €10.50; ⊙ 7.30am-11pm Mon-Fri, 9am-2.30pm Sat, Sun & hols; metro Drassanes)

SWIMMING POOLS

Club Natació Atlètic-Barcelona (4, H6; ☎ 93 221 00 10; www.cnab.org; Plaça de Mar s/n; €8/3.50; ☺ 6.30am-11pm Mon-Fri, 7am-11pm Sat year-round & 8am-5pm Sun & hols Oct–mid-May, 8am-8pm Sun & hols mid-May–Sep; metro La Barceloneta or bus 17, 39 & 64)

Piscines Bernat Picornell (1, A2; ☎ 93 423 40 41; www.picornell.com, in Catalan; Avinguda de l'Estadi 30-40, Montjuïc; over 25/15-25/child & senior €8.11/5.41/4.36, outdoor pool only Jun-Sep €4.36/3; ☺ 7am-midnight Mon-Fri, 7am-9pm Sat, 7.30am-4pm Sun, outdoor pool 10am-6pm Mon-Sat, 10am-2.30pm Sun Oct-May, 9am-9pm Mon-Sat, 9am-8pm Sun Jun-Sep; bus 50, 61 & PM)

Gay & Lesbian Travellers

Gay and lesbian sex are legal in Spain and the age of consent is 16 years, the same as it is for heterosexuals. Catalonia went a step further in October 1998 by introducing a law recognising de facto gay and lesbian couples (but not their right to marry or have children). Barcelona has a busy gay scene, as does Sitges to the southwest.

INFORMATION & ORGANISATIONS

The bi-weekly *Shanguide* is available in some gay and gay-friendly bars. Check out the Coordinadora Gai-Lesbiana website (www .cogailes.org) and GayBarcelona. Net (www.gaybarcelona.net, in Castilian). **Casal Lambda** (5, F2; ☎ 93 319 55 50; www.lambdaweb .org; Carrer de Verdaguer i Callis 10; metro Urquinaona) is a gay and lesbian social centre. The **Coordinadora Gai-Lesbiana** (4, C5; ☎ 902 120140; www.cogailes .org; Carrer de Finlàndia 45; metro

Plaça de Sants) is the city's main coordinating body for gay and lesbian groups.

Health
PRECAUTIONS

Barcelona's tap water is safe to drink (although it doesn't always taste too hot, and most locals prefer the bottled stuff), and food preparation is fairly hygienic. Heat and humidity might be a problem in summer – wear a hat and loose, comfortable clothing, and drink plenty of fluids.

MEDICAL SERVICES

At the time of research, reciprocal health agreements between EU nations were expected to change in 2005, when a European health card will be introduced. Medical costs in Spain are fairly average by European standards, and perhaps a little cheaper than in Germany and Switzerland. Travel insurance is advisable to cover any medical treatment you may need while in Barcelona. Hospitals with 24-hour accident and emergency departments:

Hospital Clínic i Provincial (4, E3; ☎ 93 227 54 00; Carrer de Villarroel 170; metro Hospital Clínic)

Hospital del Dos de Mayo (4, G1; ☎ 93 507 27 00; Carrer del Dos de Maig 301; metro Hospital de Sant Pau)

Hospital de la Santa Creu i de Sant Pau (4, G1; ☎ 93 291 90 00; Carrer de Sant Antoni Maria Claret 167; metro Hospital de Sant Pau)

DENTAL SERVICES

If you require emergency dental treatment you will have to head to one of the many private clinics around town. There is nothing particularly cheap about dental treatment in Barcelona. The **Clínica Dental Davos** (5, C1; ☎ 93 412

66 33; Carrer de Pelai 44; 🕙 9am-1pm & 3-7.30pm Mon-Fri, 9am-1pm Sat Oct-Jun, 9am-1pm & 3-7.30pm Mon-Fri Jul-Sep; metro Catalunya) has a 24-hour emergency service (☎ 93 301 33 80).

PHARMACIES

Some 24-hour pharmacies:
Farmàcia Clapés (5, D3; ☎ 93 301 28 43; La Rambla 98; metro Liceu)
Farmàcia Torres (4, F4; ☎ 93 453 92 20; Carrer d'Aribau 62; metro Universitat)
Farmàcia Álvarez (6, C5; ☎ 93 302 11 24; Passeig de Gràcia 26; metro Passeig de Gràcia)

Holidays

Jan 1	New Year's Day
Jan 6	Epiphany
Mar/Apr	Good Friday
Mar/Apr	Easter Monday
May 1	Labour Day
May/Jun	Dilluns de Pasqua Grande (day after Pentecost Sunday)
June 24	Feast of St John the Baptist
Aug 15	Feast of the Assumption
Sep 11	Catalonia's national day
Sep 24	Festes de la Mercè (five-day festival for co-patron saint Nostra Senyora de la Mercè)
Oct 12	Spain's National Day
Dec 6	Constitution Day
Dec 8	Feast of the Immaculate Conception
Dec 25	Christmas Day
Dec 26	St Stephen's Day (Boxing Day)

Internet

Barcelona is full of Internet centres. Some offer student rates and also have deals on cards for several hours' use at reduced rates.

INTERNET SERVICE PROVIDERS

Most global ISPs have dial-in codes in Spain – download a list of them before you leave home. Otherwise, you can open an account with a local ISP (if you have your own computer) or rely on Internet cafés.

INTERNET CAFÉS

BBiGG (5, E2; ☎ 93 301 40 20; www.bbigg.com; Carrer Comtal 9; per 24 mins €1.30, per hr €2-2.50, membership incl discount rates €6, 30-day unlimited pass €25; 🕙 9am-11pm Mon-Sat, 10am-11pm Sun; metro Urquinaona)
easyInternetcafé (6, B6; ☎ 93 412 13 97; www.easyeverything.com; Ronda de l'Universitat 35; unlimited access per day/week/month €5/7/12; 🕙 8am-2am; metro Catalunya). There's another **branch** (5, C5; ☎ 93 318 24 35; La Rambla 31; 🕙 8am-2.30am; metro Liceu) at La Rambla 31.

USEFUL WEBSITES

The Lonely Planet website (www.lonelyplanet.com/subwwway/) offers a speedy link to many of Barcelona's websites. Others to try:
Ajuntament de Barcelona (Barcelona Town Hall) www.bcn.es
Barcelona.com www.barcelona.com
Barcelona On-Line www.barcelona-on-line.es

Lost Property

If you lose something around town, try the city lost-property office, **Objectes Perduts** (5, E4; ☎ 010; Carrer de la Ciutat 9; 🕙 9am-2pm Mon-Fri; metro Jaume I). For things lost on public transport, try **Centre d'Atenció al Client** (4, F4; ☎ 93 318 70 74; metro Universitat), at the metro stop. For lost property in taxis try ☎ 93 223 40 12.

Metric System

The metric system is standard, and like other continental Europeans, Spaniards use commas in decimals and points to indicate thousands.

TEMPERATURE

$°C = (°F - 32) ÷ 1.8$
$°F = (°C \times 1.8) + 32$

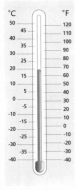

DISTANCE
1in = 2.54cm
1cm = 0.39in
1m = 3.3ft = 1.1yd
1ft = 0.3m
1km = 0.62 miles
1 mile = 1.6km

WEIGHT
1kg = 2.2lb
1lb = 0.45kg
1g = 0.04oz
1oz = 28g

VOLUME
1L = 0.26 US gallons
1 US gallon = 3.8L
1L = 0.22 imperial gallons
1 imperial gallon = 4.55L

Money
CURRENCY

Spain's currency is the euro. There are seven euro notes in denominations of €500, €200, €100, €50, €20, €10 and €5. The eight euro coins are in denominations of €2 and €1, then 50-, 20-, 10-, five-, two- and one-cent pieces.

TRAVELLERS CHEQUES

Travellers cheques can be cashed at any bank or currency-exchange office (watch the commissions, though). **American Express** (5, D4; ☎ 93 342 73 11; La Rambla dels Caputxins 74; ☺ 9am-midnight daily Apr-Sep, 9am-9pm Mon-Sat Oct-Mar; metro Liceu) is centrally located.

CREDIT CARDS

Visa and MasterCard are the most widely accepted credit cards in Spain. Small hotels and restaurants sometimes do not accept cards.

For 24-hour card cancellations or assistance, call:

AmEx	☎ 900 994426
Diners Club	☎ 901 101011
MasterCard	☎ 900 971231
Visa	☎ 900 991124

ATMS

Automatic teller machines (ATMs) are scattered liberally across the city. A plethora can be found along La Rambla and on most main streets of the central Eixample.

CHANGING MONEY

Banks generally offer the fairest rates and lowest commissions. Bureaux de change (look for the *canvi/cambio* signs) open longer hours but can offer less favourable rates and sometimes charge hefty commissions.

Newspapers & Magazines

The national *El País*, slightly left of centre, includes a daily supplement devoted to Catalonia, but the region has a lively home-grown press, too. *La Vanguardia* (with a good listings supplement on Friday) and *El Periódico* are the main local Castilian-language dailies. The latter also publishes an award-winning Catalan version. The more conservative and Catalan nationalist–oriented daily is *Avui*. Catalan daily *El Punt* concentrates on news in and around Barcelona. A plethora of international press is available at main central city newsstands, especially along La Rambla.

Post

Correus (Correos in Castilian; ☎ 902 197197; www.correos.es, in Castilian), the national postal service, has its **main office** (5, F5; ☺ 8.30am-9.30pm Mon-Sat, 9am-2pm Sun; Plaça d'Antoni López; ☺ 8.30am-9.30pm Mon-Sat, 9am-2pm Sun;

metro Jaume I) just opposite Port Vell. A handy **branch** (6, C4; Carrer d'Aragó 282; ☷ 8.30am-8.30pm Mon-Fri, 9.30am-1pm Sat; metro Passeig de Gràcia) lies just off Passeig de Gràcia. *Segells* (stamps; *sellos* in Castilian) are also sold at most *estancos* (tobacconists' shops).

POSTAL RATES
A postcard or letter weighing up to 20g costs €0.52 from Spain to other European countries, and €0.77 to the rest of the world. The same would cost €2.71 and €2.96 respectively for *certificado* (registered) mail.

Radio
The Spanish national network Radio Nacional de España (RNE) has several stations, of which RNE 1 (738 AM; 88.3 FM in Barcelona) has general interest and current affairs. Among the most listened-to rock-and-pop stations are 40 Principales (93.9 FM), Onda Cero (94.9 FM) and Cadena 100 (100 FM).

Those wanting to get into Catalan can tune into Catalunya Ràdio (102.8 FM), Catalunya Informació (92 FM) and a host of small local radio stations.

Telephone
A local phone call from a public phone will cost €0.24 for five minutes. Telefónica's blue and green public phones are scattered across the city. Most take coins and Telefónica phonecards.

PHONECARDS
Telefónica phonecards can be purchased in €6 and €12 denominations from tobacconists and post offices. Cut-rate phonecards for cheap international calls are also available from many tobacconists and some newsstands. Quality varies enormously, so shop around a little. Some Inter-

net centres also provide cut-rate international-call facilities.

MOBILE PHONES
Spain uses the GSM cellular phone system, compatible with phones sold in the rest of Europe, Australia and most of Asia, but not those from North America and Japan (unless you have a tri-band handset). Check with your service provider that they have a roaming agreement with a local counterpart. Making and receiving calls with your home mobile phone in Spain can be costly.

COUNTRY & CITY CODES
The city code (including the 9) is an integral part of the number and must always be dialled, whether calling from next door or abroad. The codes are:

Spain	☎	34
Barcelona	☎	93

USEFUL NUMBERS

International access code	☎ 00
International directory inquiries	☎ 11825
International operator & reverse charges (collect)	
Europe	☎ 1008
rest of world	☎ 1005
Local directory inquiries	☎ 11818

Television
Most TVs in Barcelona receive seven channels – two from Spain's state-run Televisión Española (TVE1 and La 2), three independents (Antena 3, Tele 5 and Canal Plus), the Catalan regional government station (TV-3) and another Catalan station (Canal 33). You may well also pick up local city stations, Barcelona TV and Citytv, and the music station Flaix (a local version of MTV).

Time

Barcelona standard time is one hour ahead of GMT/UTC. Daylight saving is practised from the last Sunday in March to the last Sunday in October.

Tipping

Diners are not expected to tip in addition to restaurant service charges, but it is common to leave a small amount, say €1 a person. If there is no service charge, the customer might consider leaving a 10% tip. In bars, Spaniards often leave any small change as a tip; often it's only €0.05 or €0.10. Tipping taxi drivers is not common practice, but you should tip the porter if you stay at a higher-end hotel.

Tourist Information

Several tourist offices operate in Barcelona. The city's **general information line** (☎ 010) is also handy, although you may have a bit of trouble getting hold of an English-speaker. The main tourist offices:

Oficina d'Informació de Turisme de Barcelona (3, B3; ☎ 807 117222, from abroad ☎ 93 368 97 30/1; www.barcelona turisme.com; Plaça de Catalunya 17-S – underground; ⊙ 9am-9pm; Ⓜ Catalunya) There are branches in the **Barri Gòtic** (5, E4; Plaça de Sant Jaume; ⊙ 9am-8pm Mon-Fri, 10am-8pm Sat, 10am-2pm Sun & hols; metro Jaume I), **Estació Sants** (4, D5; Plaça dels Països Catalans; ⊙ 8am-8pm daily Jun-Sep, 8am-8pm Mon-Fri, 8am-2pm Sat, Sun & hols Oct-May; metro Sants Estació) and the **Aeroport del Prat arrivals hall** (⊙ 9am-9pm). **Palau de la Virreina arts information office** (5, C3; ☎ 93 301 77 75; La Rambla de Sant Josep 99; ⊙ 10am-8pm Mon-Sat, 11am-3pm Sun; metro Liceu)

Regional tourist office (6, B2; ☎ 93 238 40 00; Passeig de Gràcia 107; ⊙ 10am-7pm Mon-Sat, 10am-2pm Sun; metro Diagonal)

Women Travellers

There is an indigenous problem with domestic violence against women in Spain, but Barcelona shouldn't present any specific difficulties for female travellers. The vibe in the city is less macho than it once was, and cases of harassment are few. That said, you should still exercise the same caution you would in any city and be careful which bars and clubs you frequent after dark (and especially when leaving them).

LANGUAGE

Barcelona is a bilingual city, and the local Catalan and Spanish (to be precise, Castilian – known as Castellano to the Spanish) are spoken by just about everyone. This section is based on Castilian. Where necessary, the masculine and feminine endings (usually 'o' and 'a' respectively) for words and phrases are given.

Basics

Hello.	*¡Hola!*
Goodbye.	*¡Adiós!*
Yes.	*Sí.*
No.	*No.*
Please.	*Por favor.*
Thank you.	*Gracias.*
You're welcome.	*De nada.*
Excuse me.	*Perdón.*
Sorry/Excuse me.	*Lo siento/ Discúlpeme.*
Do you speak English?	*¿Habla inglés?*
I don't understand.	*No entiendo.*
How much is this?	*¿Cuánto cuesta esto?*

Getting Around

Where is (the metro station)?	¿Dónde está (la parada de metro)?
I want to go to...	Quiero ir a...
Can you show me (on the map)?	¿Me puede indicar (en el mapa)?
When does the ...leave/arrive?	¿A qué hora sale/llega el...?
bus	autobús/bus
train	tren
metro	metro
I'd like a ticket...	Quisiera un billete...
one-way	sencillo
return	de ida y vuelta

Accommodation

Do you have any rooms available?	¿Tiene habitaciones libres?
a single room	una habitación individual
a double room	una habitación doble
a room with a bathroom	una habitación con baño
How much is it...?	¿Cuánto cuesta...?
per night	por noche
per person	por persona

Around Town

I'm looking for...	Estoy buscando...
a bank	un banco
the cathedral	la catedral
the hospital	el hospital
the police	la policía

Eating

Breakfast	desayuno
lunch	comida
dinner	cena
I'd like the set menu.	Quisiera el menú del día.
Is service included?	¿La cuenta incluye servicio?
I'm a vegetarian.	Soy vegetariano/a.

Time, Days & Numbers

What time is it?	¿Qué hora es?
today	hoy
tomorrow	mañana
yesterday	ayer
morning	mañana
afternoon	tarde
evening	noche
Monday	lunes
Tuesday	martes
Wednesday	miércoles
Thursday	jueves
Friday	viernes
Saturday	sábado
Sunday	domingo
0	cero
1	uno/una
2	dos
3	tres
4	cuatro
5	cinco
6	seis
7	siete
8	ocho
9	nueve
10	diez
100	cien/ciento
1000	mil

Health

I'm...	Soy...
diabetic	diabético/a
epileptic	epiléptico/a
asthmatic	asmático/a
I'm allergic to...	Soy alérgico/a a...
antibiotics	los antibióticos
penicillin	la penicilina

Emergencies

Help!	¡Socorro!
Call a doctor!	¡Llame a un médico!
Call the police!	¡Llame a la policía!
Where are the toilets?	¿Dónde están los servicios?
Go away!	¡Váyase!
I'm lost.	Estoy perdido/a.

Index

See also separate indexes for Eating (p125), Sleeping (p126), Shopping (p126) and Sights with map references (p127).

A

accessories 62
accommodation 96-102, *see also* Sleeping index 126
air travel 112
Aire 93
Ajuntament 38
ambulance services 116
Antic Hospital de la Santa Creu 33
antiques 60
apartments 97
Apolo 90
aquarium 14
Arc de Triomf 38
architecture 38-40, 108-9
    Catalan Gothic 12, 23, 32, 38
    contemporary 105
    Gothic 39, 40
    Modernista 17, 24, 26, 27, 38, 39, 42, 47
    Romanesque 31, 32
Arena Madre 93
art 36-7
    Catalan 11, 28
    contemporary 28-9
    Gothic 11
    pre-Columbian 28
    Romanesque 11
art galleries 27-31
ATMs 119

B

Bar Marsella 84
Bar Pastís 84
Barça 21
Barcelona Head 36
Barcelona Pipa Club 84
Barri Gòtic 6
bars 84-7
basketball 94
beaches 33, 50, 85
Bellesguard 38
bicycle hire 29, 51, 115
Bikini 90
Boadas 84
boat travel 43, 113
Bocayma 84
bookstores 59-60
breakfast 68, 102
Buda Barcelona 84
bullfighting 95
bus travel 112, 114
business hours 52, 66, 115
business travellers 75

C

cable car 29, 44
Café Que Pone Muebles Navarro 85
Café Royale 85
CaixaForum 27
Camp Nou stadium 21, 94
Capella d'En Marcús 31
car hire 114
car travel 114
carnaval 83
Carnestoltes 83
Casa Almirall 85
Casa Batlló 17
Casa Calvet 38
Casa de l'Ardiaca 38
Casa de les Punxes 38
Casa Museu Gaudí 27
Casa Vicenç 34
Casablanca 89
Cascada 25
castellers 95
Catalan flag 103
Catedral 15
Cavalcada dels Reis 83
CDLC 85
Centre de Cultura Contemporània de Barcelona 27
Centre d'Interpretació i Acollida 20
chemists 118
children
    baby-sitting 44
    entertainment 33
    restaurants 43, 72
    shopping 64
    sights & activities 42-4
churches & cathedrals 31-2, *see also* individual entries
cinemas 88-9
Circuit de Catalunya 95
Ciutat Vella 6
climate 115
clothing shops 53-5
clubs 87-8
coffee primer 77
Columbus, Christopher 13, 15, 22, 35, 40
consulates 116
CosmoCaixa 42
costs 66, 96
craft shops 60
credit cards 119
crowds 30
cuisine 67
culture 108
currency exchange 119
customs regulations 113

D

Daguiri 85
dairy bars 66, 70, 75
Dalí, Salvador 49, 110
dance 92-3
David i Goliat 36
day trips 49-50
dental services 117-18
department stores 61
design stores 56-7
Dia de Sant Jordi 83
Dia per l'Alliberament Lesbià i Gai 83
Diada 83
Diagonal Mar 6, 37
Dietrich Gay Teatro Café 93
disabled travellers 115
discount cards 7, 29, 40, 115-16
districts 6
Divendres Sant 83
Dockers 85
Dona i Ocell 36
Dot Light Club 86

E

economy 104, 107
Edifici Fòrum 37
El Born 6
El Desconsol 36
El Fòrum 6
El Fossar de les Moreres 12
El Raval 6
electricity 116
embassies 116
emergencies 116
entertainment 82-95
    costs 82, 88, 92, 94, 95
    listings 82, 88
environmental issues 106
Església de Betlem 31
Església de Sant Pau del Camp 31
Església de Sant Pere de les Puelles 32
Església de Santa Anna 32
Església de Santa Maria del Mar 12
Església de Santa Maria del Pi 32
Espai Gaudí 16
Espai Urbà 41
etiquette 106

F

Farmàcia Nordbeck 38
Feria de Abril 83
Festa de la Música 83
Festa Major de Gràcia 83
Festa Major de la Barceloneta 83
Festa Major de Sants 83
Festes de la Mercè 83
Festes de Santa Eulàlia 83
Festes dels Tres Tombs 83
Festival del Grec 83
Festival International de Jazz de Barcelona 83
festivals 83

Figueres 49
Filmoteca 89
Fira de Santa Llúcia 83
fire services 116
flamenco 91-2
food 66-81, *see also* Eating index opposite
food & drink stores 57-8
football 21, 94
Franco, General 105
Fundació Antoni Tàpies 27
Fundació Joan Miró 18
Fundación Francisco Godia 28
funfair 43

G

Galería Maeght 28
Galería Olímpica 28
Gat 36
Gaudí, Antoni 8-9, 27, 35, 41, 109
gay travellers 93-4, 98, 100, 117
gifts 56-7
Girona 49
Golondrina Excursion Boats 43
government 106-7
Gràcia 6, 34
Gran Teatre del Liceu 38, 92
gyms 116

H

Harlem Jazz Club 90
health 117-18
history 103-5
holidays 118
Homenatge a l'Exposiciò Universal del 1888 37
Homenatge a Picasso 25
homewares 56-7
Hospital de la Santa Creu i de Sant Pau 39
human-castle builders 95

I

Icària Yelmo Cineplex 89
Imax 89
Internet access 65, 118
itineraries 7

J

Jamboree 91
Jardí Botànic 33
Jardins de Mossèn Costa i Llobera 33
Jazz Sí Club 91
jewellery 62
Jewish quarter 45, 49

L

La Barceloneta 6
La Boîte 91
La Dama del Paraigua 37
La Font Màgica 43
La Paloma 88

La Pedrera 16
La Rambla 19
La Rambla del Raval 33
La Ribera 6
La Sagrada Família 8-9
La Tinaja 86
La Vinya del Senyor 86
L'Anella Olímpica & Estadi Olímpic 39
language 121-2
L'Aquàrium 14
L'Auditori 92
left luggage 113
L'Eixample 6, 33
Les Gens Que J'Aime 86
lesbian travellers 93-4, 117
L'Espai 92
L'Estel Ferit 37
literature 59
Lladró 65
Llotja 39
London Bar 86
López, Sergi 89
lost property 118
L'Ou com Balla 83
Luz de Gas 91

M

magazines 119
Manzana de la Discordia 17, 39
markets 34, 63
medical services 117
Méliès Cinemes 89
menú del día 71, 73
Mercat de l'Abaceria Central 34
Mercat del Born 39
Metro 93
metro travel 113-14
Mirablau 86
Mirador del Rei Martí 13
Miró, Joan 18, 36, 37, 110
mobile phones 120
Mochima 85
monasteries 23, 50
money 115, 119
Montjuïc 6
Montjuïc Teatre Lliure 93
Montserrat 50
Monument a Colom 40
Moog 87
Mosaic de Miró 37
Mostra de Vins i Caves de Catalunya 83
motor sports 95
motorcycle travel 114
Mulberry Cemetery 12
Museu Barbier-Mueller d'Art Precolombí 28
Museu d'Arqueologia de Catalunya 28
Museu d'Art Contemporani de Barcelona 28
Museu de Carrosses Fúnebres 41
Museu de Cera 43
Museu de Ceràmica 29

Museu de Geologia 29
Museu de la Xocolata 43
Museu de l'Eròtica 41
Museu de les Arts Decoratives 29
Museu de Montserrat 50
Museu de Zoologia 29
Museu del Calçat 41
Museu del Cinema 49
Museu del Futbol Club Barcelona 21
Museu del Perfum 30
Museu d'Història de Catalunya 30
Museu d'Història de la Ciutat 13
Museu Egipci 30
Museu Etnològic 30
Museu Frederic Marès 30
Museu Marítim 22
Museu Militar 30
Museu-Monestir de Pedralbes 23
Museu Nacional d'Art de Catalunya 11
Museu Picasso 10
Museu Tèxtil i d'Indumentària 31
museums 27-31
mushrooms 41
music stores 59-60
music venues 90-1, 92-3

N

neighbourhoods 6
New Chaps 94
newspapers 119
Nit del Foc 83
noise 7, 99

O

Olympic Games 28, 29, 36, 39
opera 92-3
Otto Zutz 87

P

paella 73
Pailebot Santa Eulàlia 22
painting 110
Palau Dalmases – Espai Barroc 86
Palau de la Generalitat 40
Palau de la Música Catalana 24, 93
Palau del Baró Quadras 40
Palau Güell 26
Parc d'Atraccions 43
Parc de Collserola 33
Parc de la Ciutadella 25
Parc d'Espanya Industrial 33
Parc Güell 20
parking 114
parks & gardens 20, 25 33-5, 39
Parlament de Catalunya 25
Passeig Marítim de la Barceloneta 33
passports 113
Pavelló Mies van der Rohe 40

Peix 37
perfume 62
pharmacies 118
Picasso, Pablo 10, 26, 110
Pitín 87
Plaça Braus Monumental 95
Plaça de Catalunya 34
Plaça de George Orwell 34
Plaça de la Vila de Madrid 34
Plaça de Rius i Taulet 34
Plaça de Sant Felip Neri 35
Plaça de Sant Jaume 35
Plaça de Sant Josep Oriol 35
Plaça de Sant Just 35
Plaça de Santa Maria
    del Mar 35
Plaça del Pi 35
Plaça del Rei 35
Plaça del Sol 35
Plaça dels Àngels 35
Plaça Reial 35
planning 115, 118
Poble Espanyol 40
police services 116
politics 106-7
population 104
Port Olímpic 6
Port Vell 6
postal services 119-20
Punto BCN 94

R
radio 120
Rambla, La 19
restaurants 66-81, *see also*
    Eating index below

road rules 114
Roman settlement 13, 34, 38, 42

S
Sala Tarantos 91
sales 53
Salo del Tinell 13
Salvation 94
Sant Ponç 83
sardana 90
Sauna Casanova 94
senior travellers 116
Setmana Tràgica 32
shopping 52-65, *see also*
    Shopping index 126
shopping bus 61
Sitges 50
sleeping 96-102, *see also*
    Sleeping index 126
solo visitors 86
Sonar 83
Soniquete 91
Spanish Civil War 32, 105
sport 94-5
statistics 104
Sutton Club 88
swimming pools 117

T
Tablao de Carmen 92
tapas 66, 69, 75, 76, 77, 78, 79,
    80, 81
tax refunds 52
taxis 114
Teatre Lliure 93

Teatre-Museu Dalí 49
Teatre Nacional de Catalunya 93
Telefèric 44, *see also* cable car
telephone services 120
Temple del Sagrat Cor 32
Temple Romà d'Augusti 42
Terrrazza 88
theatre 92-3
theft 7
time 121
tipping 121
Toros Taquilla Oficial 95
Torre Agbar 42
Torre de Collserola 40
tourist information 29, 121
tours 51
train travel 112-13, 114
travel passes 113
travellers cheques 119
TV 120

V
Va de Vi 87
vegetarian restaurants 69
Verdi 89
Verdi Park 89
visas 113

W
walks 45-8, 50
wine 79
women travellers 121

Z
Zoo de Barcelona 44

EATING

Abac	75	Ciudad Condal	78	L'Ou com Balla	77
Agua	81	Comerç 24	76	Maoz	71
Agut	69	Cometacinc	69	Margarita Blue	71
Alkímia	78	Comme-Bio		Mauri	78
Attic	68	(La Botiga)	76	Ménage à Trois	71
Bagel Shop	69	El Cafetí	74	Merendero de la Mari	81
Bar Celta	69	El Paraguayo	70	Mesón del Café	72
Bar Central	73	El Xampanyet	76	Organic	75
Bar Kasparo	73	Elche	74	Philippus	72
Biblioteca	73	Elisabets	74	Pla	72
Biocenter	73	Els Quatre Gats	70	Pla de la Garsa	77
Botafumeiro	80	Estrella de Plata	76	Restaurant Pitarra	72
Ca L'Isidre	74	Flash Flash	80	Rita Blue	75
C'al Estevet	73	Granja Dulcinea	70	Santa Maria	77
Cafè de l'Acadèmia	69	Granja Viader	75	Semproniana	78
Cafè de l'Òpera	68	Hofmann	76	Set (7) Portes	77
Cafè Zurich	68	Jean-Luc Figueras	80	Shunka	72
Cal Pep	75	La Cereria	70	Sol Soler	80
Can Culleretes	69	La Dida	78	Speakeasy	79
Can Solé	81	La Flauta Mágica	77	Specchio Magico	80
Casa Calvet	78	La Singular	80	Taktika Berri	79
Casa Leopoldo	74	L'Atzavara	78	Torre d'Alta Mar	81
Centre Cultural Euskal Etxea	75	L'Hivernacle	77	Tragaluz	79
Cerveseria Catalana	78	Los Caracoles	70	Vaso de Oro	81

SLEEPING

Alberg Mare de Déu de Montserrat	102	Hotel California	100	Hotel Jardí	101
Hostal Central	102	Hotel Casa Fuster	97	Hotel Majèstic	97
Hostal Gat Raval	102	Hotel Claris	97	Hotel Mesón de Castilla	101
Hostal Levante	102	Hotel Colón	98	Hotel Neri	98
Hostal Oliva	102	Hotel Comtes de Barcelona	97	Hotel Omm	98
Hostal Palacios	100	Hotel Continental	100	Hotel Onix Rambla	101
Hostal Windsor	100	Hotel Duques de Bergara	99	Hotel Oriente	99
Hotel Arts Barcelona	97	Hotel D'Uxelles	100	Hotel Peninsular	102
Hotel Astoria	100	Hotel España	100	Hotel Ritz	98
Hotel Axel	98	Hotel Gran Via	101	Hotel San Agustín	99
Hotel Balmes	100	Hotel Hispanos Siete Suiza	101	Park Hotel	101
Hotel Banys Orientals	100	Hotel Inglaterra	99	Pensió 2000	102

SHOPPING

Adolfo Domínguez	53	El Corte Inglés	61	L'Illa del Diagonal	61
Altaïr	59	El Ingenio	64	Lladró	65
Antinous	59	El Magnífico	57	Loewe	62
Antonio Miró	53	El Triangle	61	Majorica	65
Arlequí Màscares	64	Elephant	60	Mango	54
Armand Basi	53	Els Encants Vells	63	Marc 3	56
Art Montfalcon	56	E-male	54	Mercat de la Boqueria	63
Bad Habits	53	Escribà	58	Mullor	64
Bagués	62	Etnomusic	60	Norma Comics	65
Bd Ediciones de Diseño	56	Farrutx	54	Obach	65
Bulevard dels Antiquaris	60	FNAC	61	Papabubble	58
Bulevard Rosa	61	Forvm Ferlandina	62	Planelles	57
Caelum	57	Ganiveteria Roca	56	Próleg	60
Camper	53	Gemma Povo	60	Roser-Francesc	55
Casa del Libro	59	Germanes García	60	Sephora	62
Casa Gispert	57	Gotham	60	Sestienda	65
Castelló	59	Gothsland Galeria d'Art	60	Tactic	55
CD-Drome	59	J Murrià	58	Taller de Lencería	57
Cereria Subirà	64	Joaquín Berao	62	TincÇon	57
Collector's Corner	62	Joguines Foyè	64	Tot Formatge	58
Come In	59	Josep Font	54	Vila Viniteca	58
Cuca Fera	64	La Condoneria	64	Vinçon	57
Custo Barcelona	54	La Portorriqueña	58	Wah Wah	60
Dom	56	Laie	60	WORKcenter	65
Dos i Una	56	L'Estanc de Laietana	65	Xampany	58
Drap	64	L'Herboristeria del Rei	65	Zara	55
Du Pareil au Même	64				

Sights Index

Sight	Page	Map Ref
Ajuntament	38	(3, B3)
Antic Hospital de la Santa Creu	33	(5, C3)
Arc de Triomf	38	(5, H1)
Barcelona Head	36	(5, F5)
Bellesguard	38	(4, C1)
CaixaForum	27	(1, A1)
Capella d'En Marcús	31	(5, G3)
Casa Batlló	17	(6, B4)
Casa Calvet	38	(4, G3)
Casa de l'Ardiaca	38	(3, B1)
Casa de les Punxes	38	(6, C2)
Casa Museu Gaudí	27	(4, E1)
Casa Vicenç	34	(4, E2)
Cascada	25	(5, J3)
Catedral	15	(3, B2)
Centre de Cultura Contemporània de Barcelona	27	(5, B1)
Centre d'Interpretació i Acollida	20	(4, E1)
CosmoCaixa	42	(4, C1)
David i Goliat	36	(4, J4)
Dona i Ocell	36	(4, D5)
El Desconsol	36	(5, J4)
El Fossar de les Moreres	12	(8, B3)
Església de Betlem	31	(5, C2)
Església de Sant Pau del Camp	31	(5, A5)
Església de Sant Pere de les Puelles	32	(5, G1)
Església de Santa Anna	32	(5, D1)
Església de Santa Maria del Mar	12	(8, B3)
Església de Santa Maria del Pi	32	(5, D3)
Espai Urbà	41	(5, E4)
Farmàcia Nordbeck	38	(4, G3)
Fundació Antoni Tàpies	27	(6, B4)
Fundació Joan Miró	18	(1, B1)
Fundación Francisco Godia	28	(6, C4)
Galería Maeght	28	(8, B2)
Galería Olímpica	28	(1, B2)
Gatz	36	(5, B4)
Golondrina Excursion Boats	43	(4, G5)
Gran Teatre del Liceu	38	(5, C4)
Homenatge a l'Exposició Universal del 1888	37	(5, H3)
Homenatge a Picasso	25	(5, H4)
Hospital de la Santa Creu i de Sant Pau	39	(4, G1)
Jardí Botànic	33	(1, B2)
Jardins de Mossèn Costa i Llobera	33	(4, G6)
La Dama del Paraigua	37	(5, J5)
La Font Màgica	43	(1, A1)
La Pedrera	16	(6, B3)
La Rambla	19	(5, D2)
La Rambla del Raval	33	(5, B4)
La Sagrada Família	8	(4, G2)
L'Anella Olímpica & Estadi Olímpic	39	(1, B2)
L'Aquàrium	14	(4, H5)
L'Estel Ferit	37	(4, H5)
Llotja	39	(5, F5)
Manzana de la Discordia	39	(6, B4)
Mercat del Born	39	(5, G4)
Mirador del Rei Martí	13	(3, C2)
Monument a Colom	40	(5, C6)
Mosaic de Miró	37	(5, D3)

Sight	Page	Map Ref
Museu Barbier-Mueller d'Art Precolombí	28	(8, B1)
Museu d'Arqueologia de Catalunya	28	(1, B1)
Museu d'Art Contemporani de Barcelona	28	(5, B2)
Museu de Carrosses Fúnebres	41	(4, H3)
Museu de Cera	43	(5, D5)
Museu de Ceràmica	29	(4, B4)
Museu de Geologia	29	(5, H3)
Museu de la Xocolata	43	(5, G3)
Museu de l'Eròtica	41	(5, D3)
Museu de les Arts Decoratives	29	(4, B4)
Museu de Zoologia	29	(5, H3)
Museu del Calçat	41	(3, A2)
Museu del Futbol Club Barcelona	21	(4, B5)
Museu del Perfum	30	(6, B4)
Museu d'Història de Catalunya	30	(5, G6)
Museu d'Història de la Ciutat	13	(3, C3)
Museu Egipci	30	(6, C4)
Museu Etnològic	30	(1, B1)
Museu Frederic Marès	30	(3, C2)
Museu Marítim	22	(5, C6)
Museu Militar	30	(1, C2)
Museu-Monestir de Pedralbes	23	(4, A3)
Museu Nacional d'Art de Catalunya	11	(1, B1)
Museu Picasso	10	(8, B1)
Museu Tèxtil i d'Indumentària	31	(8, B1)
Pailebot Santa Eulàlia	22	(5, D6)
Palau de la Generalitat	40	(3, B3)
Palau de la Música Catalana	24	(5, F1)
Palau del Baró Quadras	40	(6, B2)
Palau Güell	26	(5, C4)
Parc d'Atraccions	43	(4, C1)
Parc de Collserola	33	(4, A1)
Parc de la Ciutadella	25	(5, J3)
Parc d'Espanya Industrial	33	(4, D5)
Parc Güell	20	(4, E1)
Parlament de Catalunya	25	(5, J4)
Passeig Marítim de la Barceloneta	33	(4, J5)
Pavelló Mies van der Rohe	40	(1, A1)
Peix	37	(4, J4)
Plaça de Catalunya	34	(5, D1)
Plaça de George Orwell	34	(5, D4)
Plaça de la Vila de Madrid	34	(5, D2)
Plaça de Rius i Taulet	34	(7, B3)
Plaça de Sant Felip Neri	35	(3, A2)
Plaça de Sant Jaume	35	(3, B3)
Plaça de Sant Josep Oriol & Plaça del Pi	35	(5, D3)
Plaça de Sant Just	35	(5, E4)
Plaça de Santa Maria del Mar	35	(8, A3)
Plaça del Rei	35	(3, C2)
Plaça del Sol	35	(7, B2)
Plaça dels Àngels	35	(5, B2)
Plaça Reial	35	(5, D4)
Poble Espanyol	40	(1, A1)
Salo del Tinell	13	(3, C2)
Telefèric	44	(4, G6-H5)
Temple del Sagrat Cor	32	(4, C1)
Torre Agbar	42	(4, H2)
Torre de Collserola	40	(4, A1)
Zoo de Barcelona	44	(5, J4)

FEATURES

Restaurant Pitarra	*Eating*
L'Auditori	*Entertainment*
Bar Marsella	*Drinking*
La Sagrada Família	*Highlights*
El Corte Inglés	*Shopping*
Galeria Olímpica	*Sights/Activities*
Hotel Majèstic	*Sleeping*

AREAS

	Beach, Desert
	Building
	Land
	Mall
	Market
	Other Area
	Park/Cemetery
	Sports
	Urban

HYDROGRAPHY

	River, Creek
	Water

BOUNDARIES

	International
	Ancient Wall

ROUTES

	Freeway
	Primary Road
	Secondary Road
	Tertiary Road
	Lane
	One-Way Street
	Mall/Steps
	Tunnel
	Walking Path
	Walking Trail/Track
	Walking Tour

TRANSPORT

	Airport, Airfield
	Bus Route
	Cable-Car, Funicular
	Ferry
	General Transport
	Metro
	FGC
	Rail
	Taxi Rank
	Tram

SYMBOLS

	Bank, ATM
	Christian
	Embassy, Consulate
	Hospital, Clinic
	Information
	Internet Access
	Monument
	Mountain, Volcano
	Parking Area
	Point of Interest
	Police Station
	Post Office
	Ruin
	Swimming Pool
	Zoo, Bird Sanctuary

24/7 travel advice
www.lonelyplanet.com